to a Veteran!! you enjoy story!! Don Doc

DOC
A COMBAT MEDIC'S STORY

by

Don and Shawn MacSwan

hope you enjoy the book

ISBN: 978-0-359-42517-4

Printed by LULU Publishing

www.lulu.com

Printed in the United States of America

I would like to dedicate this book to the men and women that have fought and died in the combat of war for the United States of America and her allies. It is my hope that this book will give you a better understanding of the combat soldier and a greater appreciation of our freedoms.

ACKNOWLEDGMENTS

I would like to thank Patrick Dimagard and Roy Moseman for their irreplaceable support, and my father, Don MacSwan who made this book possible.

Foreword

Several years ago I began recording my father's account of the Vietnam War, separating his memories into chronological chapters, tightly formed around the deaths of his dearest friends. My father, Doc, began confiding in me at a young age about the horror of war. When I was young his stories focused on the greatest friends he ever knew, men like Tom Ziehm, Moose Johnson, Roy Moseman, Billy Don Kennington, and Ting, their Vietnamese scout. Always present in my father's oral traditions were his leaders—Platoon Sgt. James Williams and Lt. William Dimagard, whom you will come to know.

As I grew older and my mind matured the stories became more in depth—revealing to me the descriptions I needed to help paint a picture of the true horror my father endured. Much of my work was tirelessly implementing historical, cultural and statistical information, but perhaps the greatest challenge for the two of us, were the many nights in the hunting cabin, watching my father painfully read my final drafts.

I am a rogue historian at best, but the men in this book are real. To the families of the men wounded and killed in action: it is my prayer that they will all be together again, and I can only hope I have portrayed their loved ones well.

My passion for the Vietnam War has conceived in me a great thankfulness for my gift of freedom, one which we are all forever indebted to the American Soldier. I have written this book with the conviction of knowing my life could not have come into existence had it not been for the men that poured out cover fire for my father as he gave aid to dying and wounded soldiers.

At 46 years old I have experienced much in this life. If today was my last day, I would still be thankful for the years I have had; knowing that I am an old man in comparison to the young men, woman and children that have died and will die in the combat of war. With a humbled spirit, I present to you my father's story.

**"When I die, I will go to Heaven
For I have spent my time in hell."**
(Author Unknown – found written on the back seat
of a bus in Cambodia)

Contents

Merry Christmas

In the year 1968 I could have died in Vietnam. My life is owed to the keepers of my survival. This is a true story about my personal fight for life over death and the horrific fear, pity, sadness and anger that dwelled inside me. The terror changed me for life, leaving me with a bitter taste for spoiled America. Even today, when I hear people talk about white privilege, I feel anger inside. But greater than the terror and fear was the brotherhood of men who fought and died beside me, many of whom took their last breaths in my arms.

Today, while watching the world news on television, I sometimes smile at the sight of American soldiers fighting the war on terror—all of us part of the same confident brotherhood, cool as ice, wearing designer sun glasses, eating food out of cans, writing letters to home and giving candy to the children. When I see an American soldier carrying a child to safety I know how that soldier feels, clinging to the only thread of innocence in a Godforsaken land—a land turned into a moonscape of bomb craters with the bodies of the dead littering the ground. It was the suffering of the children that bothered me the most.

In Vietnam, over 50 years ago, I made my 'Right of Passage', having fought with the greatest friends I will ever know in my lifetime. Together, we rode into the jungles and rice fields of Vietnam on the horses of the Army Air Calvary, by way of the Huey helicopter, and snaked through the perilous Mekong Delta aboard the gunboats of the Navy's Task Force 117, the Mobile Riverine Force.

At the center of everything was trying to survive and make it home again. In every war that has been fought since the history of mankind, the vacant glazed eyes of death and the fear-stricken glares of critically wounded men have remained the same. As a Combat Medic I stared into the face of death often, and now in my age it seems the screams of the dead and wounded will never leave me. I recall the memories and the horror most often when I am sitting for hours on end, alone in one of my deer stands. I think it is common for most of us combat veterans to dive into the depths of our memory when all is quiet and we're able to hear the voices of our prayers.

This is my account, Don (Doc) James MacSwan, having served the United States of America in the year 1968, in the Republic of Vietnam. I was a Combat Medic for the Army, in the 4th Battalion, 47th Infantry Regiment of the 9th Infantry Division, Charlie Company—2nd Platoon.

I flew out to Vietnam on Christmas Eve 1967 from Buffalo, New York, on a cold blustery night. Back home, under the melody of "Silent Night, Holy Night," my wife and loved ones prepared for a candle-lit service inside a small brick church. St. John Lutheran was nestled in a quiet little town called Wheatfield, located twenty miles north of the city of Buffalo. It was a farming town, standing on the edge of urban expansion, and the people there relied heavily on the land and its inhabitants for survival. Throughout the month of November, during hunting season, freshly killed deer could be seen hanging from trees. Like so many other rural towns across America with tightly knit volunteer fire halls, churches and American Legions, the Town of Wheatfield was not exempt from the draft card, nor was I.

My flight into Vietnam was an out-of-body experience, like I was looking at myself through an unbreakable piece of glass, helpless and unable to shatter the glass and stop the unfolding nightmare. As we neared Tan Son Nhut airport in the city of Saigon, two fighter jets glided smoothly next to the wings of the bulky jetliner. The pilots warned; we had to make a steep descent to the runway to avoid rocket and mortar attack aimed at us by the Viet Cong. The pilot continued on, assuring us that passenger jets were designed for much more than the family trip to Disney Land. Seconds later, we plummeted toward the earth sending my stomach on a roller coaster ride. I looked out my window and noticed the two fighter jets were mimicking our every move, holding tight, seemingly just a few feet off our wing tips. After a minute of plunging toward the earth, in one fluid motion, the fighters disappeared back into the cloudless skies over Vietnam. The pilot nosed back the plane hard, tweaking and stressing the flying structure to its limits, and we touched down on the tarmac.

I stepped off the plane and was smacked in the face with the relentless heat of the sun. The humidity was similar to that of breathing in a plastic bag and each breath was thick with jet and diesel fuel. A soldier greeted us saying, "Merry Christmas, it's 110 degrees, welcome to the Nam." U.S.O. women welcomed us, dressed in skimpy red and white shorts, with Santa Claus hats on their heads. The women's faces were glossy in appearance, ready to break into a sweat. With obligatory smiles hiding their discomfort, they gave me a handkerchief to wipe my own sweaty head.

I boarded a bus destined for the 90th Replacement Center, which was for the arrival of new infantry. The bus was a dull and awful blue, covered in a thick coat of sandy dust. Steel bars sheltered the windows, bringing the reality of war to my attention. The ride to the replacement center was sobering for me, opening my eyes to a whole new world: the cancerous poverty of the Vietnamese people. The village streets were narrow and dusty with pigs and chickens walking on and across the road. I remember thinking how fortunate Americans were, with paved streets, shopping malls and happy suburban cookouts.

The South Vietnamese people were mostly humble farmers and fishermen, usually living on the shores or close to one of the hundreds of waterways. Near the villages and cities the shores were populated, but beyond the urban areas the land was vast, with much of it inhabited only by tangled jungle, thriving green grasses, inundated fields, snakes, insects and animals.

Long before the arrival of American forces, the Vietnamese made thousands of canals that criss-crossed the entire delta using them for trade and transportation. Even today, there are few places in the delta where a person can travel two hundred yards without hitting a waterway. Near cities and villages, the brown waters of the Mekong were dense with people in sampan boats. They carried coconuts, fruits, vegetables and fish. Floating markets huddled together in the water like floating shopping malls.

The people endured the hardships of war for hundreds of years, but under the shadow of suffering and poverty the land was rich, sustaining the inhabitants who suffered on it. The full might of the United States military stood in the heart of it all.

Our American forces were like a skyscraper in a small country town.

The dust from our bus fell on the villagers and their straw, mud-floored homes, also known as hooches. From a distance the landscape of Vietnam looked like a paradise of misty highlands, lush deltas and the sandy beaches of the South China Sea, but the land was stained in blood from wars that spanned more than a thousand years.

I made it to the Replacement Center after a long bumpy drive. My eyes were wide, filled with questions and fear. That night, the famous Rachel Welch and Bob Hope were putting on a show in a stadium filled with hundreds of GI's screaming and gawking over the beautiful Ms. Welch, but I never made the show. I was almost too tired to untie my boots, it was late, and I was exhausted from the heat. The slightest movement of brushing my teeth was a chore. I stared at the ceiling, lying in my bunk, listening to men cry themselves to sleep more than 10,000 miles away from home.

I spent a few days at the 90th Replacement Center, mostly in a classroom listening to some guy tell us what to do and what not to do in Vietnam. From the Replacement Center I was flown to a massive dusty knoll of a base camp, built in the middle of the Mekong Delta, some 90 miles south of the city of Saigon. The dusty knoll was called Dong Tam. From the air it looked like a dry dessert in the middle of a vast green landscape, but as my plane circled and descended, I could see it was a massive city-fort of wooden buildings, sandbagged bunkers, tents, towers, roads and all the modern weapons the United States of America could afford. In Vietnamese the term Dong Tam means "United Hearts and Minds," symbolizing both the American and Vietnamese people.

Dong Tam served as a headquarters base camp for the joint operations between the Army's 9th Infantry Division, 2nd Brigade and the Navy's Task Force 117; together they made up the Mobile Riverine Force. The base was located 4 miles west of the city of My Tho, in the Dinh Tuong Province. In 1967 construction on the base began by dredging up sand and silt from the river bottom and mounding it on the chosen location. The work was vigorously started on 400 acres of enemy infested land, in the middle of the Mekong Delta, in preparation for the quick assembling of the Mobile Riverine Force. It stood beside the Song My Tho River, which is one of the many branches of the Mekong River itself. The building site was encircled by dense jungle, green grass and rice paddies, which were perfect terrains for the Viet Cong resistance.

When I arrived in 1968, Dong Tam stretched nearly 600 acres. The perimeter encircling the base was an earthen mound several feet high protected with razor sharp concertina wire. Throughout its length stood nearly 40 watchtowers made of wood, sandbags and steel roofing. Inside the perimeter, the base held an airport with a 1000-foot runway and a heliport. At the south end of the base was a manmade harbor with a channel leading out to the Song My Tho River where the boats of the Mobile Riverine Force were often anchored. The harbor had its own Navy dry-docks and was large enough to hold ocean-sized vessels. The mother ships of the fleet were APB's (self propelled barracks ships), LST's (landing ships tank) and APL's (non-self propelled barracks ships). The inlet into Dong Tam Harbor was in the southwest corner. On the east side of the inlet was the Dong Tam peninsula, also the location of the ammunitions depot. The western shore of the inlet was lined with dense jungle and fishing shacks and just beyond that ran the Kinh Xong Canal, or as we called it "Route 66", which traveled along the entire western perimeter of Dong Tam and continued north.

The 9th Infantry Division or "Old Reliables" was constituted on the 1st of August 1940, at Fort Bragg, North Carolina. They saw their first combat on December 11th 1942, in North Africa, against Germany's General Rommel. The 9th Infantry division fought in Sicily, France, Belgium, Germany and Korea. In Vietnam, the Army's 2nd brigade, 9th Infantry division and the Navy's Task Force 117 was the first joint operation between the Army and Navy since the Civil War, when Union soldiers operated on the Mississippi, Cumberland

and other rivers, utilizing an amphibious force entirely afloat.

In Dong Tam, the 9th Infantry Division was made up of thousands of GI's and officers. These men and women made up several infantry battalions: infantry (mechanized), assault helicopter companies, helicopter troop squadrons, tactical air support, a medical battalion, supply and transport, maintenance, engineers, combat engineers, military police, Army Rangers, scout dog platoons and military intelligence. There was a chemical detachment, an air force weather squadron and artillery battalions. The base had its own hospital, volleyball courts, movie theatres, churches and barbershops. By the greatest of standards, Dong Tam was a fire support base and a city.

Dong Tam was the hub for the Mobile Riverine Force in 1968 and I found myself smack dab in the middle of it all. About every six weeks the 4th Battalion of the 47th Infantry rotated with other battalions. We rotated between riverine operations and air-mobile. When on riverine, I was housed on one of the APB's or APL's and when on airmobile I stayed inside the perimeter of Dong Tam, but was still very much a part of the Mobile Riverine Force.

While on airmobile, the 4th of the 47th was ordered a number of different operations. The most important was being ready to support riverine troops in the field. In one role, the airmobile battalion could be used as a blocking force, against

Viet Cong soldiers fleeing from infantry forces placed ashore by the Mobile Riverine Force. The other duties of airmobile included the security of the Dong Tam perimeter, Area of Operation missions around Dong Tam, and securing the shore across the Song My Tho River, which protected the hundreds of boats in the flotilla of the Mobile Riverine Force. These missions were often platoon-sized operations, which is about 40 men. We were also attached to the mechanized units of Bandido Charlie. While mechanized, we rode on APC's (Armored Personal Carriers) with the mission usually being the protection of Highway 4—the only paved road running through the Mekong Delta.

I reported to headquarters and recalled a feeling of security. The word "headquarters" gave me the impression I would be assigned to the hospital, far from the terrors of combat. When I heard the words 4th of the 47th Infantry I was bewildered and thought there must be a mistake. Vietnam suddenly became more real to me. It was like I was sleeping, having a nightmare, then woke up into a reality much more frightening than the dream. I knew the infantry was in combat, but had no idea of the hell that awaited me. I was still just a green, pale faced, soft skinned, outsider, walking through the dusty landscape of Dong Tam. My crisp, dark green uniforms were unstained by the pungent smelling brown muck of the Mekong and my hands were without the stain of blood. The terrifying sounds of combat or the sight and smell of the death that lay ahead of me did not yet afflict my inner soul.

Doc MacSwan outside Dong Tam holding his M-1 Carbine

Dong Tam Heliport runway.

How Am I Doc?

January, 1968:

I familiarized myself with the massive base camp. The sheer quantity of powerful weapons around me and flying above seemed immeasurable. Sidewalks of planked wood were laced between the buildings across the dry, red colored soil of the earth. With each step, the hard rubber soles of my black combat boots left a perfectly imaged imprint on the dusty ground behind me. It wasn't until monsoon season that the narrow planked, sun bleached walkways were used to avoid the thick gritty mud.

I looked in disbelief as dozens of olive green utility jeeps and canvas covered trucks raged past, churning red dust into my face. I was in the far west corner of the 600-acre encampment. One of the forty watchtowers stood on the perimeter near my barracks, overlooking hundreds of yards of rice fields, and beyond the fields, dense jungle as far as my eyes could see. The bathrooms were busy, holding the same amount of people as a two-car garage, with a dull tin roof and plank wood siding.

Human waste burned in several barrels behind the bathrooms, stifling the humid air with a foul stench. The powerful whapping turbine engines of Huey helicopters were constant; several flew over me and skittered about like birds gathering food. Inside the green oval bodies of the helicopters, I could see the pilot's heads covered by heavy metal helmets with black visors covering their eyes. The sounds of the helicopters were over taken by the piercing and ear splitting shriek of two heavy bodied F-4 Phantom jets on the 1000 ft. runway.

My barracks were like the hundreds of others in the base camp, made of lumber, with plank-wood siding and a steel roof, but it was larger than most, a two story rectangle covering several thousand square feet. The window openings were covered with aluminum screens and not glass, which could be lethal if shattered by the explosion of an enemy shell. A few yards from the entrance, every barracks on base had its own bunkers made of sandbags for the walls and corrugated steel roofing covered with even more sandbags in case of an enemy mortar attack. I didn't know it yet, but I would be spending many nights in the bunkers, huddled together with a dozen men, saturated with sweat, listening to explosions shake the earth around us.

I walked up the stairs beside the bunker, opened the door and took notice to over forty steel framed bunk beds in two perfectly aligned rows, with bright white linens covering the mattresses, neatly tucked and folded all the same way. After putting my sheets on the bed, I unpacked my newly issued clothing and placed them in a tall locker beside my bed. Everything was green: jungle fatigues, hats, underwear, handkerchiefs, towels, caps, jungle boots and bush hats. Since my permanent unit the 2nd Platoon was out on a mission, I was alone in the nearly 40 x 60 foot barracks hall. It felt strange to be in a base camp of thousands of men and women when I had an entire building to myself.

Before sleeping I wrote my first letter from Vietnam to my wife Marsha. From what I remember I slept well that night, oblivious to the horror about to befall me.

In the morning I was ordered to accompany a platoon on an Area of Operation mission outside the perimeter of Dong Tam. About forty of us stood near the razor wired gate, checking our gear, hanging grenades off our chests and securing our ammo belts. I made a final effort to organize my medical bag filled with morphine, Darvocet, tourniquets, pressure dressings, cravat bandages, scissors, scalpel, artery clamps, and several other things such as iodine for purifying water, malaria tablets, aspirin and a straw for performing an emergency tracheotomy. When I was finished, I gathered my thoughts while smoking a Marlboro cigarette and waited to move out.

We stood there after checking our gear for several minutes. I was in the middle of the platoon near the commanding officer who was a young lieutenant, clean shaved, blond hair, light skin, ready to make a name for his self. His radio operator was in front of me with no special features about his tan face. The radio covered most of his back and had a long 25 foot whip antenna, bent in half and tied down to the base of the radio, but if more radio reception was needed, the antenna and its full 25 foot length could be fully extended into the air.

It seemed everyone was smoking cigarettes, and talking about anything but the mission we were about to begin. The platoon Sergeant, a small but strong black man said, "Saddle up…lock and load." Instantly, dozens of men, including myself, pulled back the bolts of our rifles and let them slam forward, loading a bullet inside the chamber of the gun, creating a clashing metal on metal echo that lasted only seconds. Shortly after, the guard on duty opened the gate and let us out into the unknown, away from the protective confines of the massive base camp of machine gun nests, artillery cannons and thousands of soldiers. We quickly became a small force of only 40 or 50 men in a landscape of endless proportions and an untold number of enemy soldiers called the Viet Cong.

We stepped forward through the gate and it quickly closed behind us. The red earth was dry and cracking with sporadic patches of short browned grass that begged for water. The dry earth ended and we crossed a long narrow stretch of lush green grass. We began to fall into a single file line, enabling us to scale an earthen mound called a dike. These dikes traversed the entire length of the fields in several places allowing us to get across the field and escape the quagmire of mud. The Vietnamese people used them for ease of movement through the inundated rice fields; however, the most vital purpose of creating dikes was to give native farmers the ability to control the flooding of the rice fields. Regardless of the ancient intentions and construction of thousands upon thousands of mounded dikes across the Mekong Delta, the dikes were a critical means of military transportation for both man and machine.

On top of the dike, the point man for our platoon was almost halfway across when I came to the field. Like everyone else, I let the man in front of me get several yards ahead before I stepped out on the dike. Keeping distance between us in the field was critical and intended to keep our casualties limited if an explosion happened to occur, and also it gave the enemy a smaller target. I had heard the phrase many times in jungle training, "Spread it out...or one round will get you all," and it was true—nobody wanted to be walking close behind a man that tripped a booby trap.

The radio chattered quietly in front of me with unrecognizable words. Below the dike that I walked on, the mud stunk of rotten vegetation and the heat of the sun seemed to suck the oxygen out of the air. I watched the mannerisms of the men around me, moving slow and methodical, with wide eyes. Their haunted glances told me I should be afraid, but I really didn't know what to be afraid of.

After stepping off the dike, I followed the men in front of me along a drainage ditch to our left. To the right was a thin hedgerow of underbrush, tall grass and frequent pockets of palm trees that ended abruptly several hundred yards ahead by the Route 66 canal. I continued on with the trudge, one foot in front of the other and then another. My body seeped perspiration and my eyes burned with sweat. I didn't know what to look for, everything looked the same, a tree was a tree and a field was a field. The Viet Cong were not going to set up as the British Red Coats did in the 18th Century. I never wanted to see the enemy, but that was a fleeting dream for the infantry soldier in Vietnam. The reality was, eventually someone would cry out for a medic. I was scared and thought about what my actions might be when someone yelled out for me. I asked myself, "What could I say to comfort a dying man?"

After an hour of walking or "humping" as we called it, we reached the brown waters of the canal. The shoreline was dry with a thick coat of knee high grass, giving us a pleasant place to break for an early lunch, but the sun still beat down on us with great weight. Each of us grabbed a little piece of grassy earth and sat down. Some of the men talked to me, trying to feel me out as the new guy. No one was overly friendly. I leaned my head down to eat lunch, my short brown hair was saturated and sweat dripped from the end of my nose. My exposed skin was pink with sunburn and my feet were blistered and burning.

While eating my C-ration of ham and lima beans, I noticed several fishing hooches or homes along the canal with nets drying in the sun, and men and women in drab colored clothing unloading fruits, vegetables and the catch of the day. They worked at a furious pace, with mud up to their knees, handing their foods up to the women on bamboo decks stilted out over the brown water.

I finished eating my C-ration and anxiously lit a Marlboro cigarette. When I was finished smoking, I put a piece of Chicklet gum in my mouth and all of us slowly, with dragging feet, formed up as a platoon and prepared to move out. One of the squads assumed the point position of the platoon and we continued to move along the Route 66 canal. We slipped through the landscape in silence, carefully placing each step on ground laced with booby traps.

The silence was shattered. I hit the ground with my chest as an explosion in front of me sent a cloud of dust into the air. It was eerily silent for a brief second. Then someone yelled out, "We need a medic up here." I felt like all eyes were on me. I made my way up to the blast area with a pounding heart, trying to pull my medical bag from my back to my side. While running through the ranks of the platoon toward the front, I was convinced the enemy would start shooting at any moment. Bent over and running, I came upon a soldier holding the hand of a legless man lying still on his back, with no helmet, wide eyes and his face dirty and young. He was soundless, staring into a cloudless sky with eyes empty of everything but fear. Both of his legs were gone at the knees. I knelt beside him and put tourniquets on what remained of his legs. I checked his vitals and told him, "You're getting the fuck out of here."

The rest of the platoon scrambled around me to secure the area. The platoon and squad leaders barked out orders, telling men where they needed to be. The wounded man told me his feet hurt. I replied, "Hang in there man, you're gonna make it." Whapping through the air, low to the ground, with a rapid approach was a Dustoff or casualty evacuation chopper from Dong Tam. Someone popped a colored smoke grenade to reveal the Landing Zone to the incoming helicopter. The wounded man stared up at me, waiting for me to say something. "How am I Doc?" he asked. I looked down at the tourniquets I placed above his knees and couldn't tell him his legs were both gone. I could only say, "Hang in there man, you're gettin' the fuck out of here." I avoided looking him in the eyes, fearing he might realize the horrific nature of his wounds, but I could feel his glare piercing through me. We carried him to the chopper and loaded him in. There was no expression on anyone's face. I could tell some of the men were his buddies and held his hands before he was loaded into the chopper.

My chest and arms were drenched in his blood. I quickly lit a cigarette after the chopper pulled out and noticed the blood on my hands. I set down my smoke and rinsed them off with muddy water. We continued the mission with a sickness and anger in the air. The silence no longer pressed with power on me, but few words were said, like it never even happened. Unable to shake off my emotions and thoughts, I felt sick to my stomach with pity and gloom. The blood didn't make me sick; it was the suffering and waste of a human life. The mutilation tore at me the entire walk back to base camp.

With the sight of the legless man pressed in my mind I tried to sleep that night. The air was thick and humid, and the sheets absorbed my sweat. I lay on my back motionless and sticky, listening to artillery cannons rattle the earth, sending devastation to some unknown enemy location. Finally, I thought of my wife's beauty with a racing heart. Then, with thoughts of my wife and home, my heartbeat slowed. I fought my emotions all night with an exhausted body, aching legs, blistered feet and fiery, pink sunburned skin. After a hailstorm of thoughts, I slept.

The next day my spirit still nagged with gut-wrenching emotions. I had no outlet for my suffering and wanted to scream at the top of my voice, but instead I stood in silence. I told myself that this was my job and this is why I was there—it was logical thinking that helped protect my mind from the trauma. The door of innocence was slammed shut forever on me. I was shackled to the war. It was a river that would take my entire being wherever it pleased.

Chopper flight above Dong Tam and the Song My Tho River

"You Ain't Seen Shit"

January, 1968:

After my first mission, the permanent unit, Charlie Company, to which I was assigned, returned from the field and quickly filled up my barracks covered in mud up to their knees and saturated with sweat. One of the squad leaders, Sgt. Maynard, a clear spoken, light-skinned man from Virginia, told me the following day our entire battalion of over a thousand men, would be picked up in the Dong Tam harbor by boat and transferred to the USS Colleton where we would carry out riverine operations. The men around me were even more exhausted than I after three days in the field. Sleep came quickly for them, but I remember lying awake that night, wondering about many things, including the condition of the man that lost his legs. I asked myself, "Would I rather die than be so afflicted?"

In the morning, several Deuce and a Half trucks, able to carry a dozen or so men, picked us up and took our entire platoon to the harbor. In a green sea bag strapped to my shoulders, hanging the length of my back, all my personal belongings were held. The sea bag was heavy and perspiration began to show through my jungle fatigues. When we arrived at the harbor the ATC boats, aka Tango boats, were idling in the water, docked along floating piers, sending clouds of diesel fumes into the air. I stood loosely, smoking and talking, introducing myself to some of the men. The Dong Tam Harbor was a rectangular 40 acres of brown water bustling with activity. In the eastern corner, Navy personnel repaired boats I never knew existed. The boats were in dry dock, elevated out of the water, resembling army tanks more than boats, blanketed with armor plating and protected with massive protruding guns. The paint on the boats was almost black, an infamous color I came to know as, "Olive Drab Green." I was taken by the magnitude of such a great mobilization of man and machine.

I stepped down a steel rung ladder into the long narrow troop bay of the Tango boat, which was converted from the LCM-6, the same boats used on the D-Day invasion of France during World War II. My entire platoon of over forty men, with equipment, weapons and food, shuffled aboard the boat with me. We each found a place to sit on the bench seats that ran both sides of the troop bay of the 56 foot long olive green landing craft.

I looked through a watertight hatch in the aft of the boat, which led into the control center, where I could see several naval personnel getting ready for our departure. The Navy crewmen consisted of the coxswain, who drove the vessel, the boat captain, a 20mm gunner, a radio man, another manning the M-19 rapid fire grenade, a 50 and 30 caliber gunner, an engineer and also a man trained in damage control; all were trained to use the several machine guns aboard.

The boats had a top speed of about eight knots with an enormous amount of pulling power, controlled by the coxswain who had an elevated view through steel bars over the troop bay. The steel bars encased the entire boat as a measure to explode enemy B-40 rockets before entering the hull. The hull itself was also reinforced with a half inch of steel. The 30 foot long rectangular troop bay where I sat was canopied over with canvas and guarded by two, cylinder shaped 20mm cannons on the elevated control quarters. I easily recognized the Tango boats as the workhorse of the Mobile Riverine Force, similar to that of the helicopter, with the ability to transport massive amounts of infantry soldiers in and near combat zones.

We pulled out of the Dong Tam Harbor and into the slow moving stagnant waters of the Song My Tho River. On both sides of our boat, near the shorelines of jungle and fishing hooches, were countless sampan boats scurrying down river toward the floating market loaded with Vietnamese men, women, children, chickens, dogs, fruits, vegetables, fish and anything else that held value at the market place. In the early morning sun, sitting low in the water, were also several boat buses, holding dozens of shoppers seeking out the daily goods needed for their families. After we passed the commotion of the floating market, I could see our destination, which was the ocean-going sized USS Colleton resting in the largest section of the river. The ship towered with the height of any cruise liner of the modern era holding inside her length the accommodations of any city. Tied to floating piers beside the Colleton was a massive armada of assault boats, able to navigate through the narrowest and shallowest canals of the Mekong Delta, bringing an enormous amount of firepower to the doorstep of the enemy.

Platoon Sergeant James Williams, a powerfully built black man from Paducah, Kentucky, came into our birthing area making rounds talking to each of the men on a personal level. With a southern voice, he asked with genuine concern about my family back home. I told him I had a wife—and he quickly gave his empathy, telling me about his own wife, the smell of her hair, his favorite dinners she made, and the last time he saw her when they went fishing down by a river. "But not too much fishing got done," he said with a smile. Then with hands of steel, Sgt. Williams grabbed me on the shoulder, looked directly into my eyes and assured me if things got rough, I could talk to him anytime. Before walking out the watertight hatchway door, he told everyone, "Tangos will be ready at 05:00."

In the morning I grabbed my gear and M-1 carbine rifle, a short wooden stocked gun with a long 30 round banana clip. After a good look at the picture of my wife, noticing her long brown hair and hazel eyes, I left the birthing area and carefully walked down the steep flight of steps under the dim lights. Like stampeding cattle, the stairs clamored with combat boots. A dim red light shined on the barge attached to the USS Colleton. I could hardly see my feet underneath me. Through the darkness I could see only faint silhouettes of the readied assault boats tucked into the floating docks, rumbling with a cloud of diesel fumes waiting for us. It was a company-sized operation consisting of three Tango boats. We walked down the floating pier to our Tango boat, climbed in, situated our gear and hunkered up inside. There were no lights—only shadows, gut wrenching sensations and fear.

Our rumbling assault force of over ten 50 foot armored, tank-like vessels began splitting the brown waters of the Mekong. At dawn, the waters of the Mekong began to bustle around us with Vietnamese in sampan boats and there were fewer, but much larger, wooden Junker boats that resembled 20 foot, two story floating motels. Speeding past my boat on both sides were two PBR's patrol boats. At 32 feet in length they were the smallest of the assault boats in our convoy. Heavily armed with 50 caliber machine guns, and twin M-60's, the v-hulled fiberglass boats scoured the two shorelines alongside us, hunting for suspicious vessels; it was their task to pull over and search the native vessels of the river for weapons caches and verify identification cards. As they sped by, I could see at least 4 men on board and the boat itself had minimal armor, its speed was obviously its best defense.

All of the boats in our convoy were powered by twin diesel engines, including the three Assault Patrol Boats (APBs), which were considered to be the destroyers of our fleet, and one Monitor boat (aka a heavy) that was often referred to as the battleship of the Riverine Force. When the river bent, twisting through the jungle, I sometimes caught a glance of the Command and Control boat near the middle of the column, where the company commander and his officers executed our search and destroy operation.

The throttle of the diesel engines lowered, their sounds became deep, almost idling. As we turned and headed for a hostile shoreline, making known to me a helpless fear and a feeling of vulnerability when stepping out on the boat's landing ramp exposed with no cover to hide behind. Sgt. Williams told everybody, "Get ready to unass." Behind him stood our leader, Lt. William Dimagard, a tall lean man from Euclid Ohio, with a brown handle-bar mustache. His helmet was low over his eyes and Overcast, our radio operator, stood behind him, dark haired and clean-shaved, a short, stocky man.

Within seconds the entire platoon was standing with pounding hearts, gripping our rifles with white knuckles. Sgt. Williams yelled out, "Platoon…lock and load." The boat hull scraped the shoreline beneath my feet with a loud echoing sound of steel slithering through mud. I looked on either side of me outside the boat and two other Tango boats were beaching at the same time. As our boat came to a halt, the diesel engines reversed and idled up with a roaring noise, spewing fumes and bubbling water into the air, giving the boat enough power to pull off the shore quickly if attacked at the Landing Zone.

The troop bay door lowered before us and thudded on the shore. I stayed close to the man in front of me in a hurried march. Sun light hit my face and I looked over his shoulder, searching for cover on the shoreline. After quickly slipping through tall grass we took cover on the edge of a jungle. I knelt behind the biggest tree I could find and the fear loosened its grip on my thumping heart and rapid breath.

We started to execute the mission along the edge of the canal of the Mekong Delta. The platoon was divided into three squads, consisting of about ten men per squad. In each squad a man carried an M-79 grenade launcher, capable of effectively hitting a target at 200 meters. The M-79 was a single-shot, breach loaded, shoulder fired weapon with several different grenades available: buckshot for close combat or HE (high explosive) that was good for clearing a bunker complex. Another man in the squad carried an M-60 machine gun, with an effective range of 1000 meters, at about 550 rounds per minute. The remainder of the squad most often held M-16's; although some did carry shotguns or like myself, an M-1 carbine with a banana clip. Separate from the three squads was my squad, which was the command squad. It included our platoon leader, Lt. Dimagard, his radio operator, Overcast, Sgt. James Williams, Sgt. Maynard, Ting, our Vietnamese scout, and myself as the platoon medic.

When Lt. Dimagard spoke he sounded like an educated man. He graduated from St. Joseph's High School in 1963, and then enrolled at Notre Dame. He soon transferred to Cleveland State University, where his GPA exceeded 3.00, just prior to entering Officer Training School for the Army. Lt. Dimagard was an athletic man who ran cross country in school, sprinkling wheat germ in his shoes for good luck. Not only did he have a love for athletics, but he was a great academic. To prevent himself from falling asleep while studying for an important exam, he put on dress shirts and ties before hitting the books. Before arriving in Vietnam, Lt. Dimagard sent this letter home to his family:

Dear Mom and Dad,

We're finally taking the big plunge and moving out of this crackerjack box. We've got a nice house lined up for the first of next month. It's a lot closer to base and has a nice physical layout.

This cycle will graduate on the 30th. With any kind of luck I can get the 3rd of July off and head for the gulf for some R&R.

The Colonel was very pleased with my class. It was enhanced because my colleagues messed up, and, beauty is by comparison. It's good to hear the news about everybody at home. Everybody seems to be prospering. Things are dull around here and I'm really looking forward to getting orders for the Nam. It's no use wasting time around here nursing these trainees.

Four-thirty comes early in the morning,

Til later,

Love Bill

The main body of our platoon stayed near the canal. We crept through tall grass, in a spread out, staggered column with a flank squad to my right, cutting with machetes through dense jungle. From what I could recognize on the radio, I believe another platoon traveled with us further inside the tangled jungle along the edge of a rice field 200 yards away. We heard an explosion shortly after moving away from the Landing Zone, revealing our

30

presence to the enemy and leaving a man from the 3rd Platoon critically wounded. Our company commander in the 1st Platoon, back near the boats, prepared another Landing Zone for a Dustoff chopper coming in from Dong Tam. When the helicopter flew past me low over the canal, I noticed he was not alone. High above in the sky two Huey Cobras, long narrow dragonfly like choppers, provided cover. They were equipped with two rocket pods on both sides and a turreted 8 barrel mini gun below the nose cone underneath the pilot. The Huey Cobra, unlike the Huey troop carriers, was designed to fly fast, solely for protection. It was a flying battleship, able to deliver a devastating amount of firepower within seconds.

We trudged the entire day in the heat, through tall-yellowed grass, ditches filled with water, waist high mud and on dikes crossing several rice fields. The mosquitoes were pestilent and flesh eating red ants fell from the trees on some of the men. After lunch we moved through a small village of about six hooches and a small school house. The buildings were all the same with straw roofs, bamboo walls and mud floors. The adults were mostly out working, leaving the village to nearly naked children playing with broken toys and chickens and the elderly who sat motionless on the ground, watching us move through the village like ghosts.

Our sweep along the canal ended just before dark. Before eating we set up a command post near the Route 66 canal, which included Lt. Dimagard, Overcast, Sgt. Williams, Sgt. Maynard and I. Within a 75 yard radius, a perimeter of three squads and two machine gun or fire team squads surrounded our command post. With careful execution, the squads reinforced the perimeter with claymore mines encircling our entire position. Claymore mines, once detonated with a hand held device, exploded hundreds of steel balls in one direction, allowing the mine to be used in close quarters combat. In addition to the claymores, the perimeter was also protected by flares that when tripped, would illuminate and give away the enemy's position, which would then be hit by all available firepower from the squad and fire team in the immediate area.

After our position was secured I ate my dinner with some of the men from the 2nd squad. Tom Ziehm, the leader of the 2nd squad was a tall, lean, clean shaved man with a distinct powerful jaw. Tom grew up on a farm in Michigan, with a playground of endless hardwoods, cornfields and apple orchards. He made hay forts in the barn and used it as a base camp while playing guns. He remembers him and his sister running down the tractor path until they hit the oak woods at the end of their 100 acre farm where they'd catch their breath, and dripping with sweat, run back to the barnyard. There was always something to do on the farm he said, catching snakes, frogs and chickens was what he remembered most.

Beside Tom was Bruce Johnson from Minnesota, a tall, big boned guy that everyone called "Moose." Tom and Moose were in the same unit for several months before getting orders for Dong Tam. The two of them were in combat together and developed a close friendship marked by nasty insults about girlfriends, body odor, being ugly and anything else the two buddies could wing at each other. Bruce also grew up in a rural town with wide open spaces to run and play. Although not on a farm, he and his mother would walk just a couple minutes down a dirt road for fresh milk, eggs, jam and vegetables. Strangely enough, as boys they both broke their noses while having apple wars in the orchards near their homes. With three of us being from the country, we had no shortage of stories to share and took turns telling hunting tales and legends that only a small farming town could tell.

After eating, Tom and Moose went back to their squad and I returned to the Command Post (CP). The sky quickly turned dark and the jungle became silent. Lt. Dimagard worked the perimeter over the radio, checking in with the five squads. The Command Post was always designated the number six. Several times throughout the night, the radio would quietly break the silence, 2-6 to 2-1 everything all right? — the 2 representing the platoon and the following number the squad. The contacted squad returned one squelch over the radio, indicating every thing was ok. Silence then returned to the squad. At least one man in each squad watched for movement, sitting motionless through the night, searching through tangled palm trees and under brush. We not only looked for the entire body of the enemy, but also for the movement of a gun barrel or a swaying branch when the wind was non-existent.

Roy Moseman of Athens, Georgia, was also on the perimeter that night with the 1st squad. His family has a tragic, but heroic military history. His father, William H. Moseman had two younger brothers die in World War II. John Carlton Moseman was killed when a German bomb hit his LST 241 during the invasion of Salerno, Italy. Herman Roy Moseman was shot down over Nuenkirchin, Germany; he was an engineer and top turret gunner on a B-24 bomber.

Roy was tall and lean with a boyish face. He entered the service on May 2nd, 1967, after volunteering for the draft. He arrived in Vietnam sometime in October, before his 20th birthday on the 28th of the month. He didn't have a girlfriend back home so unlike many of the GI's, he didn't carry a picture of his sweetheart. When he arrived at the boats, he saw two of the most pitiful looking people he had ever seen. They were two soldiers, in from several days out in the field. The GI's were unshaven, covered in mud, smelled like shit and were as tired as they could be. He said, "They held the most emotionless faces I had ever seen. I actually got a little sick to my stomach, thinking that I would look just like them very soon."

Throughout the night at least one of us inside the CP had to stay awake and work the radio. Overcast and I leaned against the same tree while Lt. Dimagard, Sgt. Williams and Sgt. Maynard tried to sleep. Overcast, from the outskirts of Pittsburgh, Pennsylvania, was a short, dark, barrel chested man. We talked with a whisper about home and girlfriends, hunting and fishing. I closed my eyes, tired of staring into nothing but obscurity and haunting shadows. It was like I was double minded with vivid thoughts carrying me thousands of miles away back home. In a blink, with the turning of a leaf, or the ruffling of a bird, my eyes ignited wide with a racing heart. I rested my body, but like a ticking clock, my mind seldom had rest. We all had the same thoughts: high school football games, hunting, fishing and fast cars. The thought of loved ones back home was ever-present, like the air we breathed. Shrouded behind every thought, word, emotion and smile, was fear.

We woke up at daybreak. The rising sun turned the chirp of the birds on again and the light gave our tired eyes some relief from straining to see in the dark. Breakfast was in the form of C-Rations and dehydrated LRRP meals. We ate everything from chopped ham and eggs to turkey loaf meal, which included at least one serving of fruit and some sort of candy. A small pack held a plastic spoon, salt, pepper, instant coffee, creamer, two Chicklets and the all important 4 cigarettes. I looked around me and saw hardened men, bartering and trading different items, complaining about the taste of the food. Deep inside we didn't really care what the food tasted like, but it was something to do and it made it feel a little more like home. They were tough young men, but some seemed very old for their years.

We moved out with the rest of Charlie Company, only yards away from the muddy canal. It was silent with the most prevalent sound being the company commander chattering over the radio checking position. I walked behind Lt. Dimagard, one step after another, pausing and searching, then walking again. The path we walked on was cut hundreds of years before us: it was narrow, shaded by trees, barely able to support the width of two men. Shade gave little comfort in the humid air. It was an ancient land with a bitter history of war and I was just another piece of that history, walking in crisp new fatigues and sun burnt skin.

We moved slow and methodical, probing for an enemy to destroy. Our enemy consisted of two different, but unified groups: one being the Viet Cong (VC) Guerillas and the second, the North Vietnamese Army (NVA). Roy Moseman said usually our enemies were units of the 514th VC battalion. Prior to my arrival, the enemy had swelled to an estimated 82,545 fighters in the delta region. Some of them were full time combat troops and others were farmers by day and guerrillas by night. Predominantly, the weapons used by the Viet Cong were AK-47's, machine guns and B-40 Rocket Propelled Grenades (RPG's). They survived off caches of rice, dried fish and ammunition hidden in the jungles and villages. The Viet Cong were a determined force, spending weeks on end in the jungle, far from civilization. Equal to their determination was their genius - forcing us to leave nothing behind. Something as simple as an empty C-Ration could be made into an explosive device. The enemy was hated, but equally respected.

The heat radiated and sweat formed on my t-shirt, saturating a v-shape of moisture around my neck. A small white Bible was in the front of my helmet and protruding off the sides of my helmet were bug spray and a pack of Marlboros. Everything was new to me, but I was alert, taking in all the fresh smells and sounds of the jungle that were so strange to me. Tom Ziehm was on point, extremely focused on the unknown jungle ahead. Lt. Dimagard advanced with Overcast, checking in with Tom at certain intervals or when he thought things were moving too slow, often ordering over the radio, "Ziehm pick up the pace." Sgt. Williams was there, holding his AR-15 rifle which he called his "little piece of shit." Williams moved with intense caution, stark white eyes glaring out from his black skin.

About an hour before noon our methodical movement turned into a dash for thick cover. The crack of a gun blast sent a bullet ripping above our position. I was on my belly near a black man named, Sanky Thomas from Alabama. It was the first time I had ever been shot at. It sounded like a whip cracking next to my ear as the bullet went by. I listened more intently to the far distance and could hear the pop from the sniper's gun muzzle, then, when a bullet came close, I heard the cracking whip again. We waited for several minutes. A few more sniper rounds went over our heads and into the jungle behind us. Lt. Dimagard yelled out, ordering everyone to stay down. After a few minutes the sniper fire stopped but we didn't stand up and instead of just laying there, I pulled out a candy bar and ate it on my back. After waiting out the sniper fire, we stood on our feet again and moved out. Lt. Dimagard notified a neighboring platoon about the sniper's existence. A Viet Cong sniper wouldn't stay in one spot very long; otherwise, he would be encompassed and killed. Rather, he would slip back further into the jungle and wait for another opportunity to snipe.

We moved a couple hundred meters and started taking on more fire. Once again I was on my belly, breathing in the pungent smell of the Mekong. I recall being exhilarated by the sporadic fire; it reminded me of playing guns as a boy in the acorn woods back home with my twin brother. I thought, "I can handle a year of this bullshit." I looked over at Sanky Thomas, who was flat on the ground and said, "This ain't so bad." Sanky looked at me with great intent, his thin, black face usually had a half smile on it after cracking a joke, but his face lost all expression. Sanky said to me, "Doc, you ain't seen shit!" What a profound statement that would become for me.

The typical search and destroy operation lasted 2 to 4 days, sometimes more, sometimes less, depending on a number of different circumstances. Again, we formed a perimeter around the command post. We heated up dinner in our helmets, using C-4, which was a high explosive and much faster than heating tabs. Sgt. Williams sat down next to Tom and me and told us some of the do's and don'ts of the Nam. I sensed immediately that Sgt. Williams cared about the men under him. Before dark, most of us blew up our air mattresses to give a good cushion from the jungle floor. After sharing stories and insulting each other, it became silent once again and we slept off our exhaustion.

In the morning while sleeping, the tide came in and we found ourselves floating in water when we awoke. Tom and I laughed about it, but it wasn't as funny once we realized our smokes got wet. After breaking camp we loaded back into the Tango boats with the rest of Charlie Company. It was a short voyage back, and soon the massive flotilla of the Mobile Riverine Force was in full view, along with the sprawling Dong Tam base camp. With air-conditioning awaiting us, the Tango's dropped us off at the USS Colleton. After showering, the cool rooms of the ship rendered me helpless to my body's exhaustion. I had enough time to glance at my old pictures and half read a previously read letter from my wife. The mornings came quickly— too quick.

Gerald Elfman, Garcia (front) Roy Moseman, Ting, Sanky Thomas and Freeman (rear)

Doc holding his M-16 on a search and
destroy operation.

Ambush

My twin brother Jon and I were born in St. Catharine's, Ontario on September 3rd 1947. My mother was a stern religious woman and my father was a charismatic artist who had just returned from World War II. Life was simple for us in the early years, with weekends spent out on the water in a row boat, catching fish with my father, while my mother sunned her self in some extravagant English sun dress while sipping tea. My father absolutely loved the water. He took us fishing nearly every day in the summer, even though for him, it often meant long periods of time untangling fishing lures from trees, and still, he maintained a smile on his face. We called him Pops and he made it evident to us, while out on the water with his twin boys, there was no other place on earth he would rather be. Fishing and heading out on early, misty summer mornings to Georgian Bay became one of my greatest pleasures; we caught giant sized pan fish one after another.

We lived in a town called Port Dalhousie, which was historically known for its carousel. We had a big three story house with lots of places to hide, and outside, just down the street was the water, where we spent endless hours fishing and swimming. When my brother and I were 5 years old we almost drowned. If it weren't for our neighbor, Mrs. Parkins jumping in the cold waters of the port and dragging us out, we would have surely died. The rescue spread like wildfire and Mrs. Parkins was featured in the local newspaper with a photograph of the three of us, my brother and I wrapped in a big towel standing beside Mrs. Parkins.

When I was six years old, my father found work in the states and we moved outside the city of Niagara Falls, New York into a small town called Colonial Village. The road we lived on had been developed with a string of houses, but beyond that, the neighborhood was surrounded with thick hardwoods and farm fields. My brother and I grew strong, wrestling around like most brothers do, spending much of our free time outside making forts, digging foxholes and playing practical jokes. The two of us were always muddy, wet, bleeding or covered head to toe in poison ivy rash.

I remember one instance when my brother Jon wrote on the bedroom wall with black marker. When my father asked who did it, Jon denied it and I was spanked for something I didn't do. I spent the entire day inside scrubbing the walls clean. I was furious with my brother and all day while cleaning the walls I thought of ways to get back at him. The following day after I scrubbed the walls spotless, I took my mother's lipstick and wrote in big letters on the wall, "Jon did this." My father spanked me again, making me spend another day cleaning off the red lipstick. We were always arguing and beating on each other, but Jon and I were as close as any brothers could be.

Our neighbor was a big burly man by the name of Al Boness. He was a combat veteran of World War II and an avid gun collector, with plenty of wooden gunstocks lying around. In the summer months, Jon and I and our buddies played guns using Al's wooden gunstocks. Making the gunstocks more real, we taped steel pipe inside the wooden stock, acting as a gun barrel. We ran through the woods for hours, day after day, playing guns and bandaging each other up, using ketchup for blood. For special missions we used an air mattress in the grass, pretending we were in the battle of Normandy, shooting off a boat and rolling into the water to save one of our buddies. Looking back, those days almost seem to have never happened. Today many of my childhood friends are no longer alive, but in a strange way I feel those early days, running wild playing guns, helped prepare me for Vietnam. It's almost like some twisted prophecy to think the same boats I pretended to be on as a child were converted for the Vietnam War and were the very boats that would take me into combat. When we grew older, the Colonial Village gang started hunting crows, rabbits, geese and deer. I remember in my youth, the sky was black with crows and without aiming my shotgun hundreds fell from the sky.

When Jon and I neared high school my parents divorced, for irreconcilable differences I guess. We both moved in with my father and lived above a bar called the Marlboro Inn. It was a three story brick hotel, always packed with motorcycles, rowdy drunks and illicit women. Through the early morning hours my father bartended there and gave us everything he could with his earnings. In the morning, after the crowd was long gone, my father spent much of the day painting and taking photographs. My brother and I became good pool players, often hustling men twice our age. Much of our talent was learned during school hours, although we managed to go to school enough to compete in football and track. The nights were wild, sometimes ending with my father kicking the shit out of someone, and if the fight got out of control, his buddy Zolton would step in and help out. He was a devoted friend to my father, but also a cruel Russian man of enormous size and strength.

One dreadful night as Jon and I were sleeping above the Marlboro Inn, we woke up in a cloud of smoke and flames. There was no time to think or

45

grab anything and we rushed outside and stood in the road in our underwear. We watched everything we owned burn up with fire. The first two stories of the bar were saved, but our apartment on the third was destroyed to ashes, and to this day the bar still stands. Never knowing the cause of the blaze, we moved on with our lives. Luckily, my father had many friends that helped us to quickly recover from the fire, giving us dozens of boxes of food and clothing.

My brother and I were both popular in school, especially with the girls. It wasn't long before I met my future wife, Marsha Lynn Krueger. She grew up with two sisters and a brother on a 100 acre farm on the other side of town in a village called Johnsburg. We spent long hours walking through the apple orchards talking and looking out at an endless wave of wheat fields. We spent every day together that spring, but as summer approached one fateful day, I received my draft notice for Vietnam. I was a Canadian native and could have easily avoided the call to war, but like my father before me, I felt I owed it to my country and I answered my draft card.

On Marsha's parent's farm there was a massive tree that stood by itself in the middle of the wheat fields, purposefully left standing by her father and the neighboring farmer to act as a lightning rod if they were caught up in a storm while on the tractors. Underneath the shade of the ancient tree, surrounded by fields, I said good-bye to Marsha and left for boot camp. When I returned from boot camp in the summer of 1967, we married at St. John's Lutheran Church. We saw each other one last time before Vietnam after I completed medic school at Fort Sam Houston in Texas.

It is hard to believe that only five years before Vietnam I was a boy playing cowboys and indians in the back woods of Colonial Village. My bedroom floor was littered with toy soldiers and dozens of model airplanes hung from the ceiling. I argued with my buddies over "who shot who," and settled matters with a bike ride to the store, or argued it out over a glass of cold lemonade. At night we slept hard and our mothers washed our muddy clothes and while waiting for the laundry to dry, they read about some far off conflict in a place called Vietnam. Unbeknownst to many of them, Vietnam was a mud they could not clean and a blood that many mothers would never forget. My old wooden gunstocks were replaced with M-16's, the ketchup was no longer ketchup, and the oak woods had become jungle.

January 1968: Mekong Delta, Dinh Tuong Province, South Vietnam,

Nearly twenty boats traveled down the mud brown waters of the Mekong with diesel engines rumbling, cascading fumes of exhaust into the air and across the canopies of jungle. I was in one of

47

the nine Tango boats, sitting quietly, watching the shoreline pass by. Stilted hooches lined the banks with crowded pockets of Vietnamese people, but mostly it was jungle. Sampan boats floated just as they did in ancient times, sitting low in the water, loaded with people and food. Above our floating taskforce flew the battalion commander in a Loach helicopter, plotting our massive search and destroy operation underway. The further we moved into the delta, the less civilization could be seen and without the bustle of the villagers, an eerie silent feeling fell into my soul. Outside the boat was nothing but brown water, jungle and rice fields. Slowly, our convoy of boats slithered through the canal like a long serpent seeking out its prey. Quickly the canal narrowed to only 75 yards wide, bringing the dark jungle closer, making known to me an ever present fear as we approached our Landing Zone.

I sat beside Tom with a cigarette in hand, catching glimpses of fear stricken eyes surrounding me. Lt. Dimagard talked calmly over the radio. Under the rumbling engines I could hear nothing of what he was saying, but could only see his lips moving with his handle bar mustache, as he spoke into the radio phone. Some of the men prayed with folded hands and others just peered intently into nothing with dreadful eyes, preparing for possible death. I began reading a small white Bible my sister-in-law Sandy Dworzanski gave to me. Everyone in the boat began exchanging glances, but few words were said. Roy Moseman once said years after the war, "When on a Tango boat or chopper, my stomach was in knots. Anyone that says they weren't scared as hell is either lying or crazy as a bat."

Stricken with fear and unfinished prayers we reached the Landing Zone. The thought of an immediate burst of fire from the enemy while unloading was a haunting, helpless fear. Lt. Dimagard gave the thumbs up and Sgt. Williams immediately ordered, "Saddle up lock and load." The front of the boat bumped the shore and the door dropped open with Sgt. Williams yelling out, "Un-ass this mother fucker." I put the boat behind me. Filled with anxiety and adrenaline, I couldn't breathe. Our squads quickly formed a line of defense a few feet inside the tree line, lying on our bellies with guns aimed into the jungle, searching for anything that wasn't us. I knelt beside Lt. Dimagard as he studied a map and received orders from the company commander. After a brief moment the realization set in—if the Viet Cong were going to hit us, they would have attacked already. The Landing Zone was secured, stabilizing my pounding heart and racing mind. The anxiety returned when we stood up and started to move out. The 1st Platoon took the point, moving into the jungle first and my platoon moved to the right side of the 1st Platoon in a flanking position. The morning quickly became hot with the sun rising higher in the sky. A day of fighting the elements of the Mekong had begun, crossing ditches filled with stagnant, thick, brown muck, our boot treads packed with mud. We climbed out of the ditches grabbing the guy's hand in front, slipping on sludge-caked boots. Mud was smeared on our faces from wiping sweat and smacking mosquitos off. Our hands, fingernails, legs and chests were all covered in mud. Once out of the water, the sun dried us with a stench, a decaying reek that I can still smell to this day. We looked for enemy footprints, campsites and turned foliage, leaving nothing unnoticed as we moved through the jungle. The heat began to nag at me like a runny nose or a persistent cough. The canopy of jungle hung heavy over us, blocking out all direct light, but the air itself was hot. Tom was on point slipping in silence toward an open rice field. The guns we carried were extensions of our bodies, as natural as the jungle boots on our feet. Any one of us could break down our rifle and reassemble it in the dark. When walking through deep water, we held our guns high above our heads like a piece of fine china, but in combat we hammered on them like a sledge.

We came to the edge of the rice field with our bodies filthy and beaten from the heat. On our left side, a tree line cut through two rice fields and connected to another jungle several hundred yards in front of us. Sgt. Williams moved up to the point and knelt beside Tom, looking around, trying to unfold the situation before him. He was nervous, I could see it on his face and in the way he lowered himself to the ground, his head on a slow swivel, looking cautiously. We moved most of the day without incident. However, the 1st Platoon did blow up a few traps that morning, luckily no one had tripped them. I heard Lt. Dimagard listening to the other platoons over the radio. He knew the enemy was in the area, but he seemed to be cool, not showing any fear. He had a real easy walk and smooth mannerisms. Everybody liked him and his confidence.

The jungle was silent and our platoon was bunching up as we neared the field. Sgt. Williams didn't like it. I heard 1st Platoon check in over the radio, notifying Lt. Dimagard they were moving out. I watched the lead squad enter the field along the tree line, walking across a dike about 150 yards away. In an instant, the air was filled with exploding guns and cries of "Medic!" Lifeless bodies continued to be filled with enemy fire and others flailed around, gripping their wounds. Some of the men tried to escape the rain of enemy fire, but were cut down near the jungle's edge. I started moving toward the ambush and the painful screams of "Medic." My body filled with adrenaline, I moved closer, almost in a full out run toward the dead and dying men. Everything I passed by seemed out of focus, but the dying men seemed crystal clear, like I was staring through a tunnel. I was only a few yards from the field in a full out run when I was knocked off my feet by Sgt. Williams. Looking at me with an angry face, he yelled under the sounds of war, "You ain't worth shit to us dead." I moved up to the tree line beside Tom Ziehm and started returning fire toward the Viet Cong position several hundred yards across the rice field. We were all shooting, but it seemed to have no effect on the incoming fire as the men of the 1st Platoon continued to get pounded.

It ended as quickly as it started. The burst of fire was intense, but brief. The Viet Cong soon melted away into an endless landscape, giving us no time to hit them back with artillery and air support. When the ambush was over, two Huey gun ships circled the area to unleash their rockets, but they were too late. The entire firefight lasted only minutes, leaving nearly ten soldiers dead or wounded. I quickly moved to the carnage of death and began treating the few survivors of the squad. I focused my immediate attention on a man bleeding out with a critical leg wound and applied a tourniquet. Once the wounded were stabilized and evacuated, I focused on the dead. Their bullet-shredded clothing was saturated with blood. Helmets, guns, brass bullet casings and cigarette packs littered the ground. Their helmets had their hometowns, children and wives names written on them. With my hands stained in their blood, I gripped the dog tags around the necks of the bodies and quickly pulled off one of the tags, placing it in my pocket. Later I would turn the tag into the senior medic for Charlie Company and the tragic news of their deaths would soon reach their families back in the United States. They died along with the dreams of their loved ones back home. The words of Sanky Thomas echoed in my mind, "Doc you ain't seen shit;" then I rinsed the blood from my hands, thankful to be alive.

Photographs

I often look at my old photographs, the first years back from the war. My first daughter, Renee Lynn, was born soon after my return on April 5th, 1970. Several months after her birth she was stricken with the flu. She became listless, burning up with a 104 degree fever. It was a cool, star lit spring night when the paramedics arrived. My wife rode in the ambulance with Renee, her little body covered with a pink, hooded spring jacket with bunny ears bouncing as they carried her away. I followed in our blue 1969 Pontiac Firebird to Degraff Memorial Hospital in North Tonawanda, New York. Renee was handed over to the care of the nurses and doctors on staff in the emergency room. After parking the car, I anxiously smoked a Marlboro Red cigarette in a small dark courtyard beside the entrance.

Blinded by fluorescent lights, I walked back into the hospital, in constant prayer with each step. I entered through double swinging doors and saw panic in the doctor's eyes. While he packed my infant child in ice, a nurse beside him was trying to give her a bottle of milk. Her fever had reached a lethal 106 degrees. Noticing my daughter had no I.V. fluids to overcome dehydration, I became enraged, almost striking the doctor with my fist. To prevent my daughter from going into shock, I demanded her to be removed from the ice and have fluids given to her immediately. Our family doctor, Dr. Gerwick had arrived, immediately he requested to have Renee transferred to Children's Hospital in the City of Buffalo.

In Vietnam, I had felt the horrific fear of losing my own life in combat many times, but nothing compared to the torrential dread of losing my child while sitting and crying and praying in that ambulance as we made our way to Children's Hospital. I never cried so hard in my life, looking down at my daughter, her tiny head motionless, her blue eyes closed, wearing a pink Easter bunny jacket with ears. I held her tiny hand, feeling the tremendous heat of the fever penetrate the flesh of my fingers. As we reached the hospital the fluids hydrated her body and the fever began to drop. Although still a very sick infant baby, the torment of my heart began to subside. After two hours in the hospital Renee's temperature dropped to 101 degrees and continued to lower. The doctor made it clear we were lucky the fever didn't continue on for much longer or Renee would have died or suffered permanent brain damage. He then shook my hand

and told me I had saved my daughter's life by pulling her out of the ice.

A year later on May 13th, 1971, my second daughter, Sherry Lynn was born, and two years later on February 14th, 1973, my son, Shawn James was born. Then, eight years after my return from Vietnam on May 16th, 1977—the same year of our infamous Buffalo storm "The Blizzard of 77", my last child Heather Lynn came into the world. There is much I don't remember of those years, but pictures can say so much, "1000 words," I think the saying goes. The camera froze the hippie biker years, deer hunting, trips to Florida and the start of a new family. The pictures remind me of a time in life when I suppressed anger about the war and also felt moments of pure joy while watching my children grow.

When I first returned from Vietnam, it was difficult for me to form any close friendships. Old friends from before the war stopped to see me at the farmhouse, talking as if nothing had changed. In fact, although I was somewhat unaware of a change, my entire being had been transformed, I was unable to connect with many of my friends from before the war. Sometimes I wanted to be alone, but the rambling voices of old friends gave me very little silence for my own thoughts. Though I cast no blame, even my own family treated me as if the war was all over for me, pressing me with deadlines and commitments. It's strange how my youthful mind was so strong, able to block out the horrors of combat, yet at times I felt like an animal in a cage, suffering alone. It was after many years my mind weakened and the horror came back with a tighter grip and vivid recollections.

I had only been home from the war a few months when I learned that Bill Parkhill, a good friend from high school, had just returned from Vietnam. Before the war our common interests were mutual friends, fast cars, building engines and racing down country roads to avoid the police. In Vietnam, Bill flew spotter planes, locating the enemy at very close ranges, often only a few feet above the tree tops. His job was essentially to draw enemy fire out of the jungle toward his airplane and relay the enemy positions to artillery units on the ground or attack jets waiting high in the skies above him. As hard as it was for me to form friendships, with Bill it was different, our friendship was forged with the brotherhood experience of combat. Having lost many good friends in the war, men that gave their lives for us, Bill and I knew the uniqueness of those friendships we had made in combat and held no expectations for eachother of ever being able to replace those voids in our souls, the brothers we had lost.

The first time I saw Bill after Vietnam we met up at a bar called the Creekside, a small, dilapidated building, leaning hard off its foundation, slowly falling into Sawyer Creek. The creek itself was sewer water mostly, with a green slimy film in the summer months. It had taken its toll on many drunk drivers, swallowing their cars and trucks to its bottom; one man was missing all winter, but early that next summer as the creek lowered in depth, the top of his truck was exposed along with his decaying body.

After a few drinks, we took a motorcycle ride on our Harley Davidsons along the shores of Lake Ontario. As strange as it was, we rode through the winding turns along the lake at suicidal speeds, a slip away from death, and I felt no fear. We opened up to each other as much as two grown men could and we spent several hours slugging down beer and smoking grass without saying a single word. Perhaps that is why we were so close, because words didn't always have to be exchanged. The questions that weighed so heavily on our minds were mutual and couldn't always be expressed with words.

With little time to adjust to civilian life, I immediately began working for the Town of Wheatfield's Parks Department building pavilions, assembling playgrounds and cutting grass in the summer. I had a lot of unsettled energy and began restoring antique cars to harness my compulsive thoughts about the war and spoiled America. Over a period of ten years, packed with antique car swap meets, late nights and long weekends, I went on to restore a 1936 Pontiac we called "Black Beauty", a

1927 Chevrolet and finally, the last car I restored was a 1956 Chevrolet Bell Air convertible for my wife. I had spent thousands of hours restoring cars during those years, but much of the time while sanding and painting, my mind was elsewhere, thinking of those I saved and those I had lost in my arms as their medic.

My wife and I raised our children in the same house where she was raised— her parent's old farmhouse. It was a grand sized house, with tall gabled peaks, white siding and black shutters around the windows. A covered porch wrapped around two sides of the home. I spent many rainy nights under that porch, rocking in a chair, listening to thunder and watching the flashes of lightning strike the vast wheat fields surrounding our house. There were hundreds of acres for the children to run and play in. Looking back now, I think the open space of the farm helped me adjust to civilian life after the war. Sometimes I thought about the countless veterans living inside crowded city limits, trying to seek peace and quiet for their tormented souls.

I was always doing something. When not restoring cars, I spent much of my time repairing the house and barn and I always found time to play football and guns with my son and his cousins. For the girls, I dressed up their bicycles with fresh paint and tassels and built them dollhouses. The old photographs of the 70's show me as a slender built man with a mustache and long hair, covered in red stain from the barn and grit from the old cars I restored. It was a peaceful time for our family. We went to Florida every winter, seeing both Busch Gardens and Disney World, and I continued to work hard for the Town of Wheatfield, giving my earnings to the family.

There are other pictures I look back at today, me standing next to my father-in-law Hank Krueger with my first big whitetail buck. I had only been home from Vietnam for a month when Hank took me deer hunting which had always been a huge event for my wife's side of the family. As it turned out, some alone time in the woods was exactly what I needed.

During that first deer hunt, I was standing on top of a deep ravine when I heard my friend Gerry Mante yell, "Deer." My instincts were still very honed from being in combat, having only a few seconds to react to a large buck running away from me. Without a single thought of preparation, I pulled up and shot and the deer dropped in its tracks. When I walked up, I saw the bullet went straight through the rectum, taking out all the vital organs.

I hunted whenever I could. Being in the woods seemed to help ease the madness that tried creeping up on me from inside the depths of my mind. Living near the shores of the Great Lakes gave us harsh hunting weather, but it didn't matter to me, some of my most memorable hunts were during blinding Buffalo blizzards. I could sit against a tree for hours while deer hunting. When the other hunters began squirming in their deer stands and walked back to camp, I sat motionless, searching for movement, as well as searching my own soul. Most hunters repositioned themselves for comfort when a leg fell asleep, but back then, my first few years home from the war, I sat impervious to discomfort with a frozen beard, in snow, wind and rain. The infantry had taught me patience—impatience would have gotten me killed. A person's eyes have been called the window to one's soul and mine had seen far more than I thought I would have by the time I turned 21 years old.

Today as I write this, my first buck still hangs on my wall. I named the deer George, figuring a big strong deer needed a strong name. Since then I have continued the ritual of naming all the deer I have taken and memorializing them by engraving the names into small brass plates and posting them on a sliced slab of hardwood that hangs on my wall. Every Christmas my wife put a Santa Claus hat on the head mount of George. Cute as it was, my daughter Renee's first word was George. They were wholesome years, filling me with purpose and meaning in my life after coming out of a living hell and seeing so much life wasted.

The 1970's had been prosperous for our entire family, but toward the end of the decade tragedy began to have its way. I suppose all families have their wonder years to hold on to. On November 12, 1977, shortly after the infamous "Blizzard of 77," my father-in-law, Hank Krueger came home from work as the Highway Superintendent of the Town of Wheatfield. He stepped out of his truck wearing blue jeans, a warm red vest, and a black baseball cap. He took just a few steps from his green Ford pickup and died before he hit the ground from a massive heart attack. My sister-in-law, Sandy Dworzanski found him lying on his back with both arms stretched out as if making the sign of the cross. She placed my 4 year old son's Buffalo Sabres jacket on the concrete underneath his head, which left a small stain of blood on the tiny coat. Every family seems to have a king pin that holds a family together—my father-in-law, Henry Krueger was ours. I remember him as a stern, yet fair Christian man that worked hard as a farmer for most of his life and loved his deer hunting. But more than anything else on earth, he loved his family.

My own father, Ian James MacSwan, was one of the few I could talk to about the war. He and I were very close, both before and after I returned from the war. However, our bond had become even stronger, partly I think because of his own experience in combat during World War II. He was very charismatic and a brilliant painter and photographer. We had a lot of fun together fishing out on the Niagara River, catching smallmouth bass like they were going out of style. In 1978, he was diagnosed with lung cancer. My brother Jon and I remained inseparable over the years and went together to visit him often. Even on his deathbed, my father kept his sense of humor. The nurse once asked him if he wanted something to ease the pain and he replied, "No thanks, I got my own", and in fact, he did have a marijuana cigarette to smoke before he died. He always had a way of smoothing over people with his charm and witty intelligence. When his cancer had become so bad we didn't know if he would make it through the night, my brother Jon and I went into a bar across the street from the hospital and ordered two Genesee Cream Ale beers. I tried walking out of the bar, but the bartender told me I couldn't leave the bar with the bottles. I told him it was the last wish of a dying man and the bartender let us go. My brother and I sat by his bedside and finished our beers together. My father and I talked about our experiences in combat, but that night we talked about the good times and all the big fish we caught together over the years. One of the last things he told my brother and I was to look up at the sky after he died and say hello to him in the center star of the belt of Orion.

On June 28, 1978, my father lost his battle with cancer and a part of me died with him. I spent the day alone in the garage building a model truck. To this day—when my son and I head out into the deer woods together, we look up at the fall sky for Orion, he says "Hey Baba," and I say "Hey Pops." Some day if the nature of life allows it, my son will say "Hey" to us both—two men out of millions, whose lives were benchmarked by the combat of war. There are few days in the year I do not think about Vietnam. I don't think of the combat as much as I do about the men that fought and died beside me. In over 40 years of deer hunting, there has not been a single hunt I have not thought about the war and conversed with my father and God. On clear mornings my eyes are always fixed on the belt of Orion, as I wait for sunrise and the elusive whitetail deer.

In that first decade after the war, I didn't have any old photographs to ponder on, as I do now as an older man looking back at the days of my youth while raising a family. But in those years, the 1970's, sometimes while stoned or drunk, I would filter through some of my pictures that I took in Vietnam. One of my fondest photographs is of Tom Ziehm and I with our arms slung over each other's shoulders in a small village outside the city of My Tho. I thought about the many nights we spent playing cards in base camp and the endless hours we whispered back and forth inside the jungle late at night. But if I stared at that picture long enough I would recall the horror that took place in and around that same village where our photograph was taken.

Doc MacSwan and Tom Ziehm at a village
outside of My Tho.

My Tho

January 31ˢᵗ, 1968:

In the final days of January 1968, there was a cease-fire, allowing all of Vietnam to celebrate the Lunar New Year, called the Tet Holiday. The North Vietnamese Army (NVA) and guerrilla fighters chose the Tet Holiday to launch a coordinated attack on South Vietnam's urban centers. The offensive involved over 80,000 NVA and Viet Cong soldiers. In the weeks that followed, nearly 45,000 were killed. The North suffered a huge defeat, but their resolve was unchanged.

The litter of death covered South Vietnam. The United States forces grieved for the death of 1,536 soldiers and for the 7,764 that were wounded. The Army of the Republic of Vietnam (ARVN) staggered with 2,788 killed in action and 8,299 that were wounded. Perhaps the greatest tragedy of all were the deaths of 14,000 civilians and the 24,000 that were wounded. In the end, the Tet Offensive was responsible for the death of nearly 63,324 men, women and children and for leaving 630,000 homeless.

February, 1968:

As my memory has it, my battalion the 4th of the 47th, was on air-mobile and transferred back to the Dong Tam base camp. We slept in wooden barracks with mosquito canopies over our bunks, a far cry from the luxuries of the USS Colleton that held real bathrooms, showers and air conditioning. Dong Tam was never quiet. I remember the first night the Viet Cong began walking mortar rounds through the base camp in linear fashion across Dong Tam's entire length, but none of the explosions were close enough to send us running to the bunkers outside our barracks. If it wasn't enemy mortar fire, it was the 10-inch track guns or the 105 and 155 Howitzers returning fire with a smashing, deafening noise, reaping havoc on enemy targets somewhere outside the wire of Dong Tam. The concussion from the big 10-inch artillery guns shook the fluorescent bulbs loose in the barracks. No matter how hard I tried, when the Howitzers were firing it rattled our teeth with concussion, making a good night sleep impossible.

My platoon leader, Lt. William Dimagard was fresh out of officer training school. He was a good-looking man, tall, lean muscle, dark, tanned skin, strong jawed with a brown handle bar mustache wrapping around his lips. He led us with a cocky self-confidence, although his cockiness was not an unconscious reflection of his inner self; rather, he acted that way consciously, because he had to lead his men into combat. A good leader must be confident if others are to follow in their stead. Certainly, Lt. Dimagard was overconfident; he hadn't been in Vietnam long enough to see the cunning capabilities of the Viet Cong. We thought of him as a great leader, very seldom showing any fear.

Lieutenant William Dimagard (right)
with brother Patrick after graduation

One of the reasons Lt. Dimagard was a great platoon leader was his willingness to listen to men who had been in Vietnam longer than himself, men such as Sgt.Williams, who was a hardened veteran of the war, having been in horrific firefights throughout the Mekong Delta region. Sgt. Williams was a lifer, not a draftee. He was well into his 2nd tour in Vietnam and knew the capabilities, tactics and tendencies of the Viet Cong guerilla fighters and also the North Vietnamese Army. Lt. Dimagard, in all of his confidence, paid close attention to the words of Sgt. Williams.

Inside the perimeter of Dong Tam, Sgt. Williams made his rounds talking to us, showing genuine concern about our well being, asking about families, children and what we planned on doing when we got home. He was black as any man could be. A red handkerchief was usually tied around his strong neck, his head shaved. His height was of medium stature, but wide, with well-built muscularity. I could just tell he had his shit together, meaning he had all angles covered—a complete defense against anything able to harm the mind or body, which included the ability to control fear in combat and rely on sound judgment, rather than emotion.

The three platoons of our Company stood on the black tarmac and somewhere in the Mekong Delta, our 4th Mortar Platoon was being flown out to an already secured position to aid us—giving us fire support in the field. The mass of destructive power held by the 4th Platoon gave me one of the few emotional comforts in the Nam. The Bell UH-1 helicopters or (Hueys) were upon us and brought with them the familiar thumping echo. The Hueys had a maximum capacity of 10 men, a range of up to 327 miles and a crew of 4 men: the pilot in command, co-pilot, crew chief and gunner. The pilots came out of Ft. Wolters near Mineral Springs, Texas, where they flew OH-13's. After graduating flight school in Texas, they entered the Huey school for combat flight at Ft. Rucker, Alabama. In the mid to late 60's, 98% of the pilots passing combat flight school knew they were going to Vietnam. For generations of Americans, the image of a helicopter in a jungle Landing Zone could only mean one thing—Vietnam. The helicopter so dominated American operations that the conflict has been rightly called, "The Helicopter War." The helicopter airlift changed the face of warfare. During World War II, the average combat veteran saw 40 days of action throughout the year; in Vietnam, the combat veteran saw 240 days of combat. The staggering increase of engagements with the enemy was by and large, the result of air-mobility.

The "Slicks" as we called them, approached in a mid-air column and touched down before us, the tarmac on which they landed was sweltering hot. Several hundred feet in the sky above us circled two

Huey Cobra gun ships. The Bell UH-1 had gunship models, but the Cobra was the first of its class, specifically designed as a killing machine. It held a mini gun in the nose and was armed to the hilt with dozens of rockets. I waited on the flight deck with thoughts about anything but the mission ahead of me. In a way, I guess I separated my mind from the actions of my body, but my stomach was still in knots. Under the thunderous noise of the Huey's T-53 jet turbine engines, I could hear the racing thoughts in my mind. We waited to load the choppers by squad and platoon, over a hundred of us stood in the heat in a loose formation. The designated chopper touched down in front of my squad and we loaded without hesitation.

In the air my mind quickly began to focus on the Landing Zone (LZ) with very little comfort placed in the Cobra gunships flying above the airlift. Although they waited to pounce on the first threat launched against us, once we were on the ground if the enemy attacked us at close range the Cobra's firepower would do us no good. The mission ahead of us was designated a training mission. Since enemy movement had been non-existent in that region of the delta, our anxieties were relatively low. The LZ was soon in sight, looking like a tropical paradise on the front of a post card with lush, waist high green grass blowing in the wind surrounded by palm trees. But the wind was from the blades of the helicopters and the jungle was never a paradise. The pilots wasted no time dropping the helicopters down to the earth. At 100 feet, Sgt. Williams stepped outside the doors, setting one foot down on the landing skids, one hand held him from falling to his death and the other held his rifle. His red neckerchief blew with the speed of the helicopter. I edged near the door waiting to dive for cover into the waist high grass. Lt. Dimagard pulled his radio helmet off and put his field helmet on, then gave Sgt. Williams a nod to unload. Instantly, it was assholes and elbows out the doors and into the grass.

We were the first lift of infantry on the ground and quickly formed a perimeter around the LZ. The choppers flew out of sight, leaving us with the eerie silence of jungle and chirping birds. Once the LZ was secured, most of us smoked a cigarette while waiting for the second lift to arrive. Lt. Dimagard was on the radio calling out for a marking round. Seconds later, we heard the incoming shell whistle over our heads, bursting into a cloud of smoke over the nearby jungle. The marking round gave us some comfort, knowing we were under the protective canopy of artillery support. Having artillery support was as good a feeling as we could hope for in the jungle, except for the sound of the helicopters coming in to get us out and take us back to Dong Tam for a few days.

Nearly 60 men sat motionless inside the field of tall grass, the landscape silent. I finished my cigarette and threw a piece of Chicklet gum in my mouth and watched the second lift of choppers bring in the other half of our company. After a brief ruckus of helicopter turbines and rushing wind, our insertion was complete and the platoons spread out and executed a coordinated sweep of the area— better known as a "search and destroy operation." Lunchtime was spent wheeling and dealing over peaches and pound cake.

The training mission took up a large part of the day. I remember Garcia being on the mission. He was a soft-spoken Latino, very olive skin, thick mustache and dark wavy hair. His body was muscular and wide, his accent strong. The first time I met him he seemed quiet, almost timid, but I soon realized Garcia was not so much timid as he was a genuinely nice guy, often I saw him in the evenings reading a small brown Bible. Garcia was very well liked by all the men, and the more I knew him, I could see the respect the men held for him as one of the veterans of the platoon.

Sanky Thomas had me roaring with laughter that day. He and Washington, who was another black man, were teasing me as I handed out malaria tablets. "You trying to kill us again Doc... keep'n us good for this shit," Sanky rambled, with a big black southern smile. Laughing with us was another black man named Bobby Freeman from Atlanta, Georgia. He was tall and lanky and somewhat quieter than the other black men, telling jokes which were usually racial, regarding the prejudice against the black man fighting a white man's war. Lt. Dimagard was not happy with the grab ass going on, but Sanky continued to tell his jokes with a slow southern drawl, keeping a smile on his face long after a joke ceased being funny. He was very talkative, but not the least bit overpowering or annoying and the bitter jokes helped pass the countless hours spent in the exhausting heat, covered in mud, mosquito bites, ant bites, trying to peer through burning sweaty eyes. Deep inside we all knew we were the same, standing on the frontline of a war.

When the training mission was over, the airlift landed before us in a pleasant Landing Zone in the middle of a different grass field, somewhere in the Mekong Delta. We loaded without hesitation and once again we were in the air. The stretching jungle beneath me was impenetrable, divided by canals and hedgerows of palm trees lush with fruits and the fields with rice. Peasant farmers in plain clothing toiled on their land beneath us, covered by oversized straw hats. The heat of the sun was constant. Every so often a woman in brightly decorated clothes would dot the landscape in a village. In and around the villages people swarmed to catch a glimpse of the helicopters thundering over their heads. Water buffalo and pigs stood still on the fringes of the villages. Inside my helicopter the crew chief and gunner sat behind the two 30 caliber machine guns mounted on swivels in both doors. The guns were an extension of the gunner's body, their eyes wide, with shoulders resting against the stock of the gun, ready to fire. Lt. Dimagard sat behind the pilots with a radio helmet on. A dark visor covered his strong face, only his handlebar mustache and jaw line were exposed. The red handkerchief around Sgt. William's neck tossed in the wind, his hands holding an AR-15 assault rifle.

I looked at the other ten choppers in the airlift cutting through the sky without much effort. Storming across an ancient land, inhabited with such simple living people while I was enthroned in the technology of the United States Army was a powerful feeling. Today, I can still hear the roar of a sky filled with choppers, truly the villagers must have been in awe.

Ting sat in the chopper beside me. He was a Viet Cong Lieutenant who had turned his allegiance over to the United States, serving as a scout and translator for our platoon. The protection and exchange operation of former Viet Cong soldiers was known as the "Chieu Hoi" program. The Mekong Delta was Ting's backyard and he knew every village, canal and jungle that sprawled across the region. Ting could spot booby traps with ease by detecting turned over leaves and fallen trees, even browned out grass put him on high alert. Ting's knowledge was a priceless gift for our platoon and since he was often with Lt. Dimagard's command squad, he and I quickly became good friends.

The wind blew through the open doors of the helicopter, giving little comfort from the heat of the sun. As we headed back to Dong Tam, expecting a hot shower and meal, Lt. Dimagard's voice became intense over the radio. He was notified that Viet Cong movement was spotted near the city of My Tho. Our airlift changed direction in a quick sweeping motion. Suddenly, the training mission had become real. The helicopter rotors thumped with a throatier sound as the turn demanded more power from the turbine engines. We became alert like one giant air born predator. I had not yet landed under fire and recall the fear of that flight to My Tho.

We had a secure Landing Zone on Highway 4 which eased my anxiety, but before landing, I looked down at the village near our LZ and saw chaos. The villagers seemed to be in a state of panic with loud voices. Pigs and chickens ran wild across the dusty half- paved road. Once on the ground, I could taste the grit in my mouth as the helicopters quickly lifted, churning the red dirt into the air around us, enveloping all the chaos in a cloud of dust. With Lt. Dimagard and Sgt. Williams waiting eagerly beside him, Ting immediately began to translate the villager's cries. He searched through dozens of people, hoping to find a village chief or someone in authority. I looked around searching for the source of panic and chaos with my hands gripped tight to my rifle.

In the far distance, east of our position, Alpha Company was being placed on the ground and several klicks (kilometers) to the North, Echo Company's men were in position on the other side of a canal with mortar support. Ting quickly gathered the cry from the villagers and said to Lt. Dimagard, "Beaucoup VC." Lt. Dimagard then raised his hands in the air with a smirk on his face and said, "Beaucoup GI." Ting, with every seriousness his thin muscular body could muster said, "No, no, no, beaucoup, beaucoup VC." The face on Lt. Dimagard became flush with a seldom seen fear, and quickly turned to Sgt. Williams to help sift through the madness. Overcast, holding the radio unit on his back, was practically being dragged by the phone as Dimagard paced back and forth, communicating with company and battalion commanders. About twenty minutes after we landed, the noise and chaos increased once again as the choppers of Bravo Company flew in over our heads. I tried watching Bravo's choppers skim a tree line and begin their descent about a half klick away to the West, but it was late in the day, making it difficult to look into the sun.

Instantly, a wall of rockets streamed out of a tree line, smashing into Bravo Company's helicopters. We heard the screams of the men through Overcast's radio and watched four choppers engulfed in flames crash and burn into a rice field. I noticed some men jumping off the choppers before hitting the ground. My focus on the burning choppers, billowing smoke and screaming men was quickly broken as enemy mortar rounds exploded toward us and a tree line about five hundred yards away opened up with machine gun and small arms fire. Without hesitation, we swept through a small village and formed a straight-line perimeter along the road.

Women and children and pigs and chickens and water buffalo ran wild through the village and the surrounding landscape. There were women coddling their babies while lying in a ditch, filthy with mud. The earth shook and the air rocked with noise and concussion. I ran a short distance under a heavy volume of small arms fire and reached a slight mound in the earth. Soon after, the Viet Cong focused their firepower on the men of Bravo Company that survived the landing. We could hear them getting cut to pieces as they fought with only one platoon of their company. They screamed coordinates for fire support over the radio, but the enemy was too close for air support. We couldn't fire into the enemy position without hitting our own GI's. Through the chaotic sounds of the screaming villagers around me, I could still hear the distant rattling of Bravo's guns. They were pinned down behind a dike in the middle of the rice field.

Our new company commander ordered the 2nd Platoon to put on gas masks and fix bayonets. We thought, "Who the fuck is this guy?" We didn't carry gas masks. He ordered our platoon to advance toward the enemy tree line, but the moment we stood up the Viet Cong began firing on us and the order to advance into the rice field was never carried out by Lt. Dimagard and Sgt. Williams.

At dusk, a light haze of gun-powdered smoke hung in the air. The battle continued on into the dark of night, with a loud barking M-60 machine gun spitting rapidly into the Viet Cong position. The enemy's green tracers and Bravo's red tracers crossed back and forth through the night sky by the thousands with only 100 yards separating the two. We stayed buried behind a dike, knowing it would have been suicide for us to go any further toward the Viet Cong stronghold.

After nearly 1 hour of close combat, Bravo Company was low on ammunition but managed to withdraw to a greater distance from the tree line. Within minutes, F-4 Phantom jets shrieked over us and dropped napalm, turning the enemy position into orange and red burning flames as high as the trees. Shortly after, I witnessed the power of a B-52 bomber for the first time. I could not see the massive airplanes, but I heard the bombs whistling by the hundreds toward the ground. The impact of the 1000 pound bombs was mesmerizing, sending hundreds of trees into the air like burning tooth picks as chunks of mud large enough to kill a man fell to the earth. The B-52's struck three times that night, along with the Napalm and High Explosive (HE) brought in by the F-4's. The night was filled with luminous lights of fire, destruction and burning flesh. The smell of rotten eggs was in the air from the burned napalm. It became quiet on our perimeter except for the sound of Dustoff or medical evacuation choppers taking out the dead and wounded.

After checking out some minor shrapnel wounds on a couple of the men, we rested on the floor of the jungle talking about home and asking each other what we planned to do when we went home. Several times throughout night the ground trembled from distant bombs, our conversations ended and all eyes watched the hell raining down on top of the enemy.

They were all alive then. Tom Ziehm sat with his boyish face beside me holding his M-16 and Moose was holding his. Our scout Ting sat next to me. He almost always had a smile on his face and when he didn't, we knew something was wrong. Also close to my side that night was Billy Don Kennington from the mountains of North Carolina and Roy Moseman from the hills of Georgia. Garcia was there, who had taken Moseman under his wing when he first arrived in the Nam. Lt. Dimagard, Overcast, Sgt. Williams and Sgt. Maynard were also there. Williams was on his second tour in Vietnam and had seen all this destruction before. Wilbanks and Kramer, the hefty machine gunners found themselves in the nightmare. There are more, many more. Parham from New York, Donald Hensley, Michael Hanrahan, Mills, Scotty, Sanky Thomas, Bobby Freeman, Pat Schloegel, Bernard Richardson from New York, Gerald Elfman and Ed Padden, who grew up in Niagara Falls near my hometown. There was also Sgt. Wilborn, and the unforgettable Roscoe, who was running around that day saying, "They got their shit together this time." They were all alive that day, when Bravo and Alpha Company were torn up, not far from the City of My Tho.

We half slept that night, watching Alpha Company in a heated fire fight several hundred yards away, seeing only the exchange of green and red tracers. Each second and every breath brought us a bit closer to the end. No one knew how their end would unfold. For some it would be a return home realizing how spoiled Americans were after seeing, hearing, smelling and tasting the shit and urine stench the Vietnamese lived in. For others it would be their intestines spilling out of their belly. Some would lose arms and legs and others would have bullets across their chest. It didn't matter what kind of wound a dead man had—he was dead. That is what the future held for us, and we slept.

We woke up at daybreak. After listening to the distant battle overnight and feeling the B-52 strikes shaking the earth like a giant deafening alarm clock,

I hardly slept. I had never seen a full-scale battle before and when I did close my eyes, I was gripped with the images of F-4 Phantoms leaving hundreds of acres of jungle exploding and burning with bright orange flames. I wanted to sleep but kept seeing screaming soldiers, dead mothers holding their children, crashing helicopters and B-52 strikes shaking and illuminating the earth. It was both horrific and mesmerizing to see. I could not believe the power of such an army. Without sympathy, I wondered how many hundreds of Viet Cong perished.

Early that morning we swept the area where the choppers of Bravo Company went down. With a dreadful feeling I navigated my way through the scattered debris and charred helicopter skeletons. The dead and wounded had been removed, leaving only brass bullet casings and blood stained grass to silently echo the horror of the place on which I stood. Death was in the air, along with the scent of fuel. Dead Viet Cong and body parts were being counted and thrown into one of the hundreds of bomb craters. The villagers were quiet and the animals began to slowly move about, picking at the empty C-Ration cans. The morning sun brought a new day and also a new life for many. It was a dawn of new beginning, for not only the wounded and the families back home, but also the dead who were no longer in hell.

We broke for lunch inside a narrow jungle surrounded by rice paddies. I sat down beside Tom Ziehm and lit a small piece of C-4 explosive, instantly heating water for my coffee. Dripping with sweat and slapping at mosquitoes, the heat overwhelmed the land even under the canopy of the jungle. My M1 carbine rifle rested across my lap while I ate. I looked up sporadically, glancing down a small path that could afford the enemy an escape from the region—knowing that hundreds of the Viet Cong had been surrounded by two battalions of the U.S. Army and Navy.

With a thud in my heart, I looked up once again. Moving toward me down the path was my enemy, a single soldier that had been tormented by us all night. He moved low to the ground, trying to stay out of sight. Our eyes widened together, seeing each other at the same time, only a few feet apart. In unison we grabbed for our weapons and time stood still. The movements of his body were in slow motion as he lowered the muzzle of his AK-47 toward me. But I was already on him and pulled the trigger, sending several rounds into the man's chest. He was blown away from me. It felt strange, being in perfect control over my body's action. It was pure instinct I guess. He slid down a tree gasping for air and bleeding from the mouth. I was frozen with my gun still on him. His eyes widened, I could see death coming over him. He twitched and thrashed on the ground for a second or two and then life left his body. His eyes began to glass over, becoming hollow and distant. When he stopped moving and died it was like turning off a light switch; he fell limp, and in that limpness, with the speed of light, the life left his body. It was similar to the way a deer dies, when they thrash on the ground.

I knelt beside the body, blood still oozed out of the holes in a khaki shirt covering his chest. The image of him dying played through my mind. I felt sick, as emotion flooded my soul. My entire life I was raised under the Ten Commandments, "Thou shall not kill," but the army said I could. I pulled out the man's wallet and compounding my inner torment, I found a picture of his wife. It wasn't the blood or the smell of his dying body or his nothingness eyes making me sick, it was the taking of a life and the supernatural sight of a soul leaving a body.

I looked in silence at the useless body. The GI's began to slap me on the back. Their slaps felt like punches, they said, "Nice shot Doc, nice shot Doc." My nausea soon left when I realized how close I had just come to death. It was either my life or his. It was close and personal for me. In a firefight bullets are flying and hitting the enemy, but this was different; I watched my bullets enter this man's chest and saw a picture of his wife. Even today I can still see his wife's face, a young, beautiful Cambodian woman with big, almond-shaped eyes. I thought how different the enemy was from us, but also how very similar. We were both fighting in a war, far away from our families and we all died the same.

The slicks flew in and set down before us. I climbed into the chopper next to Lt. Dimagard, Sgt. Williams, Ting and a few other GI's. On the ground, the view of the carnage was limited. The villagers looked at us with faces of nothing, as if all spirit and soul had been ripped out of them. When we lifted into the air, the land revealed her wounds. The 1000-pound bombs dropped by the B-52's turned a sprawling lush jungle into ash and craters resembling the surface of the moon. The sight was sickening, but not as nagging as the sickness inside my soul. The picture of the Viet Cong soldier's wife was in the front of my mind, along with the thought that I wasn't much different than the Viet Cong.

Dong Tam was soon in sight. The massive flotilla of the Riverine Force was easily seen. PBR boats scoured the shorelines, blowing their sirens to halt suspicious vessels. Everything was business as usual. Jeeps and trucks kicked up dust. People hustled in and out of hundreds of buildings inside the base camp. Aircraft taxied the runway. Helicopters filled much of the sky. But it was not business as usual for me, for the first time I had taken a human life in the most personal way—face-to-face and eye-to-eye. It hung on me with great weight.

Sleepless Nights

The 4th of July was never the same for me after Vietnam. Every year, red, white and blue explosions fill the night sky. Parents sit with their children saying, "oooo…ah ah ah." Underneath the sound of explosions, beer is in the cooler, hot dogs are on the grill and men are holding women in their arms on the hood of a car. Behind them in the distance is the combat veteran, like myself, every explosion permeating through his body, the "National Anthem" bringing visions of sacrifice and horror. I do not see the litter of a picnic, but brass bullet casings and the dead distorted in awkward positions and brothers holding brothers. I don't always hear the fireworks that the multitudes revel in, but sounds of the past, explosions that shatter eardrums and dismember the human body. Another world is locked inside of us. They hear the music and think of the greatness of our country, and those that brought it to them. But we hear "Taps," and recall grown men crying out for Jesus in the middle of a rice field or the sands of the Middle East. And some of us touch the scars on our bodies thinking of the names of men that saved our lives.

The fathers and mothers of the dead are also there beside me. Their attic is filled: stuffed animals, clothing, fishing poles, high school diplomas and toys. Photographs are haunting and their child's favorite foods are bittersweet. They remember the day of delivery in the hospital and also the day of departure, as their child stepped on a plane going to a land from which they would never return. They hear the roar of explosions and it penetrates their soul, but pain is nothing like the silence of a childless home. What would they give to hear, "Mom or Dad" once more? These are the thoughts the fireworks on the 4th of July bring to my mind, taking me back to a real time in my life so long ago, yet seems like only yesterday.

February, 1968:

My unit returned to Dong Tam. We set down on the hot tarmac once again, where the entire mission had started. Our clothing all looked the same with mud and water stains up to the knees. Each step toward the barracks was an uncomfortable task. My feet ached. I took off my socks, revealing my shriveled, saturated, painful feet. My clothing was heavy with sweat, weighing twice its actual weight. Hot meals, cold showers and cold beer were the awaiting comforts to me and maybe some mail from a loved one.

I hit the showers and went straight to the enlisted club, healing my emotions with beer and marijuana and a couple of Darvocet pills. We played cards and talked as if nothing had ever happened that day. Late at night, in a drunken stupor, I laid in my bunk, the face of death haunting me. But the vision didn't stay very long. Enemy mortar rounds began shaking the earth, exploding with a distinct metal-splitting sound. But I was too exhausted to move to the bunker. The explosions came closer, but still I couldn't move. Finally, when it felt like the barracks was coming apart, I ran with Tom Ziehm to the bunker. While waiting out the attack I could only hear my thoughts under the smashing explosions. When I returned to my bunk, something inside me seemed to have died, but I was reminded that as a whole, I was still alive. I had made it through.

We operated out of the Dong Tam base camp for the next several weeks and like clockwork, as evening approached and the nighttime sky cascaded across the land, the earth began to tremble and we prepared for another sleepless night in Vietnam as Viet Cong mortar and rocket fire began to rain down. We were mortared for over 30 nights in a row. The Viet Cong waited for us to sleep, then hit us with a few rockets and mortars, just enough to make us run for the bunker and lose sleep. Although the bunkers were hot and nasty, eventually we stayed in them all night, sleeping as much as possible.

Ambush patrols outside the Dong Tam perimeter were also becoming increasingly hostile. We could tell things weren't right. All of the ARVN soldiers had deserted their guard posts around the hamlets and villages. On one mission we ran across about thirty bunkers that the VC had just made. Although we made little contact on that operation, we knew the enemy was all around us.

Our base camp had become a main target after the Tet Offensive. We spent so many nights under the shutter of explosions and chaos that avoiding them and running to the bunkers became as commonplace as going to the bathroom. One second we were snoring in bed, the next, running for our lives. Helicopter gun ships searched for the enemy mortar teams, but they would flee at the sound of the turbine engines. Through it all we stared at each other under deafening noise, smelling sweat and feeling the same fear. If the enemy's incoming fire wasn't keeping us from sleep, it was the outgoing Howitzer cannons shaking the base camp. It was pure exhaustion, overcome only by the threat of death.

We all had a different hometown to hold on to, but the essence of home was the same for us all. It was a thread of hope, a lifeline to a sanity that was trying to elude us. A home is a home is a home— anything but the fuck'n Nam. For Sgt. Williams part of that vision was his brand new car back home. I remember him well. Sgt. Williams had his shit together. He had a personal conviction to get his boys home. When a man was killed or wounded, Sgt. Williams took it personally. He had been in Vietnam nearly two years; he was smart and cunning in combat. Much of his knowledge was instinct, but what he learned in the field was priceless to all of us.

Sgt. Williams hung with all the GI's in base camp, shooting the shit and drinking beer. We lived like there was no tomorrow. I can see all of their faces etched in my mind, at the bar, huddled around tables, talking bullshit, underneath the music, "I gotta get out of this place, if it's the last thing I ever do." Sanky Thomas with his black talkative face was there. Moseman's southern drawl and Garcia's friendly face also come to my mind. I see myself in my youth next to Tom Ziehm, Bruce Johnson and Ting. We're all laughing, drunk, holding cards in a dimly lit bar, with Tom and I pissed off at Ting for kicking our ass in poker—we taught him a little too well. There were times of laughter, but to me there was an unspoken false sense about it all. Fake laughs and fake smiles hid the true anguish of longing to be home.

The dreaded Area of Operation (AO) missions around Dong Tam continued, and we already sent a share of our guy's home with shrapnel-filled bodies. One mission at Dong Tam I remember clearly. Our platoon was securing the perimeter of the base camp itself—we called it berm guard. The perimeter around the base was mounded high into the air with concertina razor wire running its entire length. Garcia and I were up in one of the towers that stood in increments around the perimeter when mortar fire began to fall in the distance. The enemy was so close we could see fire shooting out of the Viet Cong mortar tubes. The explosions grew closer as the enemy adjusted their fire.

On the ground, several GI's ran for the bunker and I began climbing out of the tower. The explosions were close and earthshaking, Garcia's slender body made the move to get out of the tower after me. Behind him the night was black, except the explosive bursts coming toward us. In seconds explosions and flying mud were on top of us. Skipping the last few ladder rungs, I jumped, hitting the earth hard. I was a few steps away from the bunker when a round exploded at the base of the tower. I looked through dust and debris as it settled and found Garcia lying on his back at the bottom of the ladder. I ran to his side, his eyes wide and scared as explosions continued around us. His abdomen was ripped open by shrapnel and my eyes followed a stream of intestines going from Garcia's gut through the dirt and up the ladder. I placed a dressing on his stomach and climbed the ladder. A quarter ways up the ladder, I gently began lifting his intestines in and out of the rungs, winding them up like a garden hose. I could feel Garcia's eyes watching me as I placed them in a plastic bag and secured them to his side. With eyes filled with the fear of death, he held his insides with two hands.

We loaded into a 3 quarter ton truck and aimed for the hospital. Holding his hand, looking in his eyes, I tried to reassure him with words, "Hang in there man...your gonna make it." Even with my words, Garcia knew he might die. There was little blood, but the smallest piece of shrapnel could have been vital, not to mention the risk of infection. Garcia looked up at me without a word, the truck bouncing its way toward the hospital. I asked myself, "Is he going to die?"

Not too much was said about a GI that had been wounded. Today, Roy Moseman admits he took it pretty hard. He recalls, "I really hated it, because Garcia was the one that took me under his wing, so to speak, and taught me a lot about the field. I have always wondered about him and what he is doing now." We didn't like seeing another man get wounded, but we never said much, it just wasn't something we talked about. Even though the killed and wounded weren't dwelled on, it was a good feeling to find out that someone did make it out alive. It turned out Garcia did make it. His vision of home became a reality. He lost a couple of feet of intestine and gained a scar across his abdomen, but he went home, and not in a casket.

It was about that time when Tom received a package from home. Inside were cookies and three rubber Superman figures. He gave one Superman to me and another to Bruce Johnson and kept one for himself. We called ourselves the "Super troopers." Every mission made the three of us closer. I talked with all the men, but Bruce and Tom and I confided in each other. We spent many nights sharing memories of home and our greatest fears.

Everything we did was for home and the smiling faces waiting for us. Each step through the jungle, rice paddies, banana groves and muddy canals was one more step toward home. Exploding mortar rounds had to be avoided, booby traps had to be spotted and firefights had to be fought, then maybe, we could walk up the front steps of our house again. When the mud was deep, my legs aching, my feet hurting and feeling I could no longer move on, I thought of home. Ultimate victory comes in many ways: destroying an evil empire, peaceful resolutions and the freeing of captive people. In Vietnam, the ultimate victory for us was going home in one piece; that hope of victory spawned heroic actions as great as any war. We fought for our homeland, just as the Viet Cong did.

Bandido Charlie

It has been many years since the war. I'm 71 now and hope to see my grandchildren grow big and strong. The Krueger Farmhouse where we raised the kids still stands, but the apples and wheat fields are all gone now and it seems the years have passed like a summer storm. My youngest daughter works on a labor wing in a large Buffalo suburban hospital near home. While visiting her at work, I remembered delivering the child of a young Vietnamese woman, who had been wounded during a firefight. The mission began just outside the gates of Dong Tam on Highway 4, only a few miles from the city of My Tho, where the choppers of Bravo Company were blown out of the sky.

I stood with Tom and Bruce (Moose), each of us wearing rubber Superman figures on our helmets. My helmet also held my small white Bible, and my wife's name, "Marsha" was written on it. My crisp green fatigues were beginning to fade to a mud brown, my skin was no longer pale, but dark brown, the skin on my arms almost black. We stood in the humid heat, sweating standing still, waiting for the tracks, also known as tanks. Our mission was to assist an armored unit in keeping Highway 4, the only paved road in the delta, clear of enemy threat. Highway 4 served as the main supply line for U.S. forces, crossing several villages and canals, but the constant pounding by heavy military vehicles made the road rough. The narrow, dust covered road was lined with jungle and rice paddies, providing perfect cover for the Viet Cong to mount an ambush.

A few miles away from Dong Tam, a rising cloud of dust ascended into the air. The sandy fog was like a living creature, moving closer. The cloud of dust was above the big-leafed palm trees and came with a rumbling noise, shaking the ground. The dust neared my platoon. Pressing on before the storm of fog were the tracks. It was their job to keep the road safe.

I looked at the rolling tanks and saw the silhouette of a single man. As the lead track drew closer, the figure of the man became clearer with each second. He was a light skinned, black man with wide eyes, full lips, red hair and thick freckles covering his skin. A black handkerchief wrapped around his neck and an undersized green flack vest covered his torso. Below the vest, on his side, was a scar from a shrapnel wound the size of a man's fist. He sat in a steel chair welded to the top of the tank with folded arms and tossing in the air above him was a skull and crossbones flag. The armored unit called themselves, "Bandido Charlie."

There were maybe ten tracks in all, each with a skull and cross bones flag. They were a rugged bunch of tank men, with ears strung around their necks, sliced from the heads of dead Viet Cong. Their clothes were cut off, far from military issue, faces unshaved and weathered, like having not seen a shower in weeks. It felt like I was riding with the Hells Angels of Highway 4, a vicious gang, wanting nothing more than to kill and torture Viet Cong. Their red haired leader we called "Bandido." I didn't know his name or his rank, but I was sure he bowed down to no one. He had no smile and his eyes were cold and murderous with no emotion. Although I could sense little about this crazy man, I felt a deep commitment of protection from him over his men.

I sat on top of an Armored Personal Carrier (APC) next to Lt. Dimagard and Sgt. Williams with our rifles in hand. I was scared, sitting seven feet off the ground moving at high speed. The APC's had enough room inside to hold a squad of men, but the troop bay was used for storing food, ammunition, water and clothing instead of men, since the armor piercing weapons used by the Viet Cong had a tendency to turn the troop bay into a burning inferno. We rumbled down Highway 4 with turbo charged engines at over 50 mph, a cloud of dust spewing into the air behind us. Bandido and his men had their own inner circle of communication, sometimes smirking with glaring eyes, leaving me to wonder what thoughts were behind their devious grins. At a glance, a person might think they were a disorganized bunch, but the combat of war soon proved otherwise to me.

The village of Andook stood along the highway, crowded with pigs, chickens and Vietnamese people. We rolled through the quiet ancient village, sitting on top of the tracks and holding on for our lives. The leaves on the trees stood motionless in the humid air, the animals were calm, walking slowly by the roadside. The villagers waited for our distant rumble, and in seconds we were upon them, blowing back the leaves and grass like a storm of thunder with squawking and whining animals. The villagers cursed out loud, holding up hand gestures to show their unhappiness. We covered the village in sandy grit, quickly leaving the small hamlet in a fog of disarray. Bandido sat in his steel chair, arms folded, eyes forward, never flinching; his black skull and crossbones flag blew with the speed of the tanks above his red afro hair.

We pressed further down the road, all flags blowing with the current of wind. Some tracks had quad 40 mm cannons, others had mortars mounted on top and many had 50 caliber machine guns, each manned by one of Bandido's men. The landscape returned to nothing but jungle and rice paddies. It was getting dark and the shadows began to haunt my eyes. As night settled in, we entered a dimly lit ARVN post next to a steel bridge that crossed the Route 66 canal. The building was a large wooden structure protected with concrete barriers, surrounded by razor wire. We unloaded off the tracks, Lt. Dimagard, Sgt. Williams, Ting, Tom Ziehm's first squad and me as the medic.

Ting immediately began interpreting curious children from a small fishing village beside the bridge. There was a haze of gun powder over the water, telling me artillery had found NVA soldiers or gorilla fighters in the region. Before we entered the building we heard Viet Cong yelling from the other side of the bridge, "Fuck you GI…Fuck you GI." It was eerie having the enemy taunting us so close, only a few hundred yards away.

When we entered the post, it was dark inside, dimly lit with red and green Christmas lights hanging around the tops of the walls. I could see only silhouettes and shadows of American and ARVN troops stumbling around drunk and high on drugs. Bandido and his men started drinking rice whiskey and smoking grass. I went through a small opening into a bunker and had a few drinks. I was taken by Bandido's madness and the scars on his body and his men smoking and laughing, holding up their trophies; the ears of dead Viet Cong soldiers. Bandido began telling a story with wide eyes, about a pack of wild baboons running around tearing apart villagers, a joint dangling from his lips.

We returned to the tanks, Bandido's men each with a joint in their mouth, a bottle of whiskey in one hand and a gun in the other. The engines fired up, filling the air with the familiar clouds of diesel fumes. Still feeling the effects from smoking marijuana, my balance was impaired while climbing back on top of the tank next to Dimagard and Williams. With no headlights, at high speeds on the narrow road, we headed back toward Dong Tam. The night was black; we heard only the rumble of engines.

A few miles down the road, an explosion rocked our convoy with a bright orange flash and an umbrella of dust and debris quickly rained down on us. Two tanks from the end of the convoy rushed past us, encapsulated in an invisible midnight dust that I could taste in my mouth and feel in my eyes as the particles irritated them. The tanks from the rear formed a perimeter around the heavily armed, powerful lead tank now crippled from a land mine with a broken track, like a battleship out of water.

With a furious face, one of Bandido's men came to me, intent eyes racing into mine, saying, "We got lucky Doc…sit tight." My heartbeat lowered to normal with the knowledge of having no wounded men and breathing in deep, I lit a Marlboro Red cigarette. Literally in seconds, scrambling with great speed, turbo diesel engines screaming with precision movement, Bandido Charlie rolled the wounded tank onto a new track and we were on our way again at 50 mph down Highway 4.

I hated the darkness, unable to even see the slightest forms of trees just a few feet away on either side of the road. We knew the enemy was all around us, plotting their next movement, digging holes, laying landmines, infiltrating small villages for food and supplies and searching for the perfect place for an ambush. I felt my every movement was being watched, even the cigarette that went to and from my lips. The Viet Cong could have been a few feet away, indeed they were, but we couldn't see them.

Late that night with heavy, sleepy eyes, the sight and sounds of Dong Tam were upon us. I walked through the main gate with my platoon, hit the showers and then finally my bunk, grabbing much needed rest. My eyes started to close, exhaustion overwhelming, but enemy mortar rounds began exploding around us. We ran to the bunker half asleep and as we packed ourselves like sardines in a can of sweat and body odor, we were filled with furious anger for an enemy we could do nothing but tolerate. We returned to the barracks and hit the bunks again and the explosions returned, sending us running for cover once again, half sleeping and half fearing for our lives. It seemed the enemy knew when my eyes were about to close, then the earth shook leaving everyone running for the bunker once again. The game of cat and mouse went on all night, but as dawn closed in, the Viet Cong left, giving us a few hours of sleep before the rise of the sun.

With booby traps and ambushes, the Viet Cong were a constant menace to Highway 4. The next morning, once again, we rode with Bandido Charlie a few miles outside Dong Tam; on our left flank was rice field and distant jungle, on the right flank stood a small village we had cleared the day before. In the blink of an eye all hell broke loose, two enemy rockets missed over our heads and bullets thudded the mud beside the road. Bandido's action toward the enemy was insane, but also life saving. Normally when a track unit was fired upon, they formed a perimeter and returned fire and the attached infantry dismounted and reinforced the perimeter. But Bandido did nothing of the sort. When the ambush hit, our red-haired leader pounced like a cat, charging the Viet Cong position inside a young growth of jungle a few hundred feet away. Turning off the road and into a muddy rice field, turbo engines roaring, mud and water spewing thirty feet in the air, skull and cross bone flags waving, I held on for my life. The Viet Cong position lashed out with more rockets, exploding all around us. Machine gun fire continued to hail, ricocheting off the tank between Lt. Dimagard and me. All the tank cannons lowered and opened up with quad 40's, 50 caliber machine guns and mortars; a flame thrower ignited the tree line into flames. We pressed on through their position, running over them, crushing and mulching the few survivors that didn't flee. The enemy ambush was silenced in seconds. When the fight was finished, the tree line held a few mangled enemy soldiers and one of our men was seriously wounded. I couldn't believe how quickly Bandido reacted and how well Bandido Charlie fought as one cohesive unit. They reacted like a fine tuned machine, the Hell's Angels of Highway 4. Bandido's eyes were the size of silver dollars. Bandido said with intensity, "Can you believe them mother fuckers?" He spoke as if the enemy must have been out of their minds to attack him and his boys. I can only describe Bandido Charlie one way—a bunch of tough, crazy mother fuckers.

After the ambush we heard cries from the village. Seriously wounded with a nearly severed leg, a pregnant woman cried in pain, the trauma had forced her body into full labor by the time I came to her side. The young woman kept trying to sit up and squat to give birth with her toddler screaming in one arm—I didn't know until later, but that was how Vietnamese women give birth. I delivered the child and loaded the woman with her newborn son in the back of an APC, taking her to the Dong Tam Hospital.

The following day I visited the woman. She was happy with a constant, radiating smile. I felt good inside, but was smitten with the ironies of war. We were in the middle of a combat zone, with dead bodies stacked up like fire wood—yet a birth, a new life of a child, could still bring smiles to the very people that bore the deepest scars of the Vietnam War.

The Area of Operation around Dong Tam continued to be threatened by the Viet Cong. As Roy Moseman said, "After Tet we made contact with the VC on every mission. Before Tet it was mostly booby traps and a few snipers. After Tet it was larger VC units. One of the main forces in the area was the 514th VC battalion. We were always fighting these guys. They never seemed to run out of men. We would go into an area, fight them, kill a dozen, then go back into the same area the next week and they would be there again."

The nights inside Dong Tam continued to be filled with enemy mortar fire. Sleep was almost non-existent. We could set our watches to the mortar attacks. We got up, ran to the bunker, waited it out and returned to our bunks.

With the rising sun came AO missions around Dong Tam. We slept and walked on pins and needles, not knowing if a mortar or a booby trap had one of our names on it. We scrambled through mud and water. Snipers pestered us. Leeches sucked on our bodies, jungle rot ate at our feet. Through the several weeks of bombardment, I treated many soldiers unknown to me with horrific wounds and placed several in body bags. I was in the armpit of the world and death and the cry for a medic was as certain as the dawn of the next day.

Doc MacSwan getting back from a tough mission.

Can Tho

Sgt. Williams told us the next mission was an easy one. Charlie Company had to pull security for the construction of a firebase outside the city of Can Tho, the southern most city of Vietnam. Deep inside, I knew that an easy mission could turn hot and hard in an instant. The only thing predictable about the Viet Cong was their unpredictability. The moment a soldier thinks they have figured out the enemy, they become most vulnerable.

At our barracks in Dong Tam deuce and a half trucks picked us up and took us to the flight line. Stepping out of the trucks, the morning was hot without a cloud in the sky. Huey helicopters were popping loud, overpowering our words with deafness and rushing wind. We brought all kinds of weapons: grenades, recoilless rifles, M-79 grenade launchers and anything else we could get our hands on. Formed in squads, we loaded inside the choppers. We had a love and hate relationship with helicopters, loved them when getting picked up in the jungle, but hated them when getting flown out.

The flight to Can Tho was a long one. We were in the air over two hours with Sgt. Williams next to me, red hanky blowing in the wind beside my face. I looked down at endless rows of massive bomb craters filled with muddy water interspersed with lush jungle intermittently turned to miles of ash and charred leafless trees. Nearing the city, the lifeless battlefields faded to a breathtaking tropical paradise, the beaches of the South China Sea. It was beautiful. The brown water of the Mekong filtered out into a light turquoise blue sea lined with clean white sand. Standing above it all was the City of Can Tho with hotels, shops, restaurants and paved roads. The modern city bustled with traffic, cars, bicycles and thousands of people scurrying from one place to the next.

We landed a few miles outside Can Tho and began unloading our gear. At the same time, an artillery unit was flying in. The air filled with Huey's carrying ammo crates, equipment, and men. Several massive, twin blade Chinook helicopters, with long steel cables under their bellies, hauled 155 Howitzer cannons, setting them down at our new base camp—a dust bowl that had been cleared with Agent Orange and heavy equipment. Roy Moseman was next to me on the radio with another Radio Transmitter Operator (RTO), when suddenly the radio squelched loud, turning silent. Immediately I saw the commotion increase on the ground. Men from the artillery unit yelled out, "Medic!" I ran through a crowd of people, encircling a man, cut in half at the shoulder by an ammo crate released to soon from a chopper, his body looking like it had been peeled with a can opener at the base of his neck. He turned his eyes of sorrow to mine, glazed with the face and fear of death. I leaned my ear close to his lips as he struggled to speak, with a whisper he said, "Tell Marsha I love her."

I had seen many men die unknown to me, but his wife's name being the same as my own wife helped permeate his memory even deeper in my mind. I told his buddy standing beside me the last words that his comrade struggled to say, tears were in the soldier's eyes. Walking back to my platoon through churning dust I thought, "You just never fucking know."

After unloading and checking our equipment we loosely formed up, not in boot camp type formation, but a couple of columns of straggling GI's, talking shit and smoking cigarettes. Entering the military base, people waved, cheered from windows, shook our hands and asked questions about the weapons we carried. We were treated like royalty, like freedom fighters sent to secure a city constantly being menaced by the enemy. Our living quarters for the night were polished clean, a far cry from the film of dust at the Dong Tam barracks. After putting away personal belongings, we went to the chow hall. Escorted immediately to the front of the food line, my company entered and ate like kings.

That night after drinking at the enlisted club, we went into the city of Can Tho. In the streets, young Vietnamese boys pestered us, offering everything from Pepsi, Coca Cola, heroin, marijuana, prostitutes and even a shining of our shoes. A bunch of us walked into a small boutique bar, crowded with Vietnamese women, GI's and nurses. After being in combat, we didn't give a shit about anything and began drinking and smoking grass like there was no tomorrow.

A GI by the name of Connors was with us that night, wired heavily on drugs, and picked a fight with another GI. In no time, the entire bar was a brawl of smashed bar stools and shattered windows, leaving the building in a heap of ruin. Before the military police showed up, I made an escape along with Tom, Moose and Connors, and spent the rest of the night drinking, smoking grass and listening to music. Everyone else went separate ways, some back to base camp while others shacked up with nurses and Vietnamese women. I heard that after the war, Connors eventually ended up in Japan for drug rehabilitation.

In the morning revile sounded as a call to form ranks and raise the American flag. Sgt. Williams and Lt. Dimagard gave the wake up call. The regular soldiers on base formed neat ranks to the left our company, with uniforms crisp and clean. Half of our company's men were missing, still sleeping, drunk, high or in bed with a woman. Beside the flag was a decorative cannon set up as a memorial and sleeping under the barrel of the cannon was a GI we called Junky, passed out drunk and stinking of whiskey. Those of us that did show up for revile were rough, no shirts, stinking like beer or whiskey with blood shot eyes. The base commander said we were a disgrace to the Army, but we didn't give a shit what anybody thought.

That afternoon we had water buffalo steak for lunch. Before shipping out, most of us took the rare opportunity of using an actual post office, sending out letters and trinkets acquired from the city's gift shops. Some of the men packed marijuana into china dolls to send home as precious gifts to their families—a perfect safety deposit of marijuana if they returned home alive. The choppers waited for us in a soccer field; we loaded up and were flown to a village about two kilometers away from the city.

The sun was setting, Ting talked to the villagers with an uneasy feeling saying, "Me no like," about a fishing village across the canal. As darkness fell, Ting was unconvinced about the safety of our position. Despite his uneasiness, he came back that evening with Zuday whiskey and a twinkle in his eyes. When Ting relaxed, everyone relaxed. The Zuday whiskey we drank tasted like rubbing alcohol; it was the moonshine of the Nam. In a drunken stupor, we watched across the canal. The far shore was dark, with only incense candles burning in the village windows.

Without warning, the enemy fired at us. Their green tracer bullets illuminated across the canal like thousands of tiny glowing rockets. We shot back, sending our own trail of red tracers across the canal toward them. Then silence returned and the night sky was black once again. The tension was low amongst us, knowing that even for a sizable enemy force it would have been suicide to attack an infantry company and an artillery unit. The sporadic shooting back and forth continued on, some us shot back and others didn't bother since it was such a great distance. The only casualty was an old farmer hit in the side, but I bandaged him up and sent him to a field hospital.

The villagers had finally convinced Ting that there were only a few Viet Cong in the area. Ting, with an idea and sheepish grin came to me, laughing with a snicker and said, "zit—zin", which is duck and chicken in Vietnamese. He tried saying duck and chicken, but it sounded like, "duke and chickan." He ejected two bullets from his M-1 rifle. I stared at him with wonder as he pried the bullet heads from their casings, poured out some of the gunpowder and replaced the bullet heads with cardboard wads. He put the bullets back together, telling Tom and I to follow him. We crept on our bellies through a dry grass field, not knowing where we were going or what we were about to do, except that it had something to do with ducks and chickens. Ting was beginning to snicker again, but stopped, reminding us that we had to be silent. Coming to a farmyard with chickens resting in it, we finally had a good idea what he was up to. A couple hundred feet from the yard was the farmer's hooch. We watched it cautiously. Following Ting under a fence and into the yard, the animals began to stir and crow. Quickly pulling out his gun Ting shot a chicken, stunning it with the cardboard wad. I grabbed the chicken while Ting shot another bird.

A scream of anger raged out in the distance, growing louder and louder as the farmer, in a furious frenzy, holding some sort of weapon in his hand ran toward us. In a heated rush, the three of us ran back toward the perimeter of Charlie Company with the stunned chickens regaining their senses, forcing us to stop and break their necks. The farmer was hot on our heels, holding a pitchfork, cursing and screaming. As the farmer neared us he became quiet, realizing he was an old man chasing three men with assault rifles, holding only a pitchfork.

We stayed by the canal for a couple more nights, exchanging aimless gunshots with the Viet Cong. I always liked telling that story to my son and his friends from school. We were all living then, during the most difficult days of our lives, yet we found a way to create humor. I can still see Lt.

Dimagard, Ting, Tom Ziehm, Sgt. Williams, Roy Moseman, Bruce Johnson, and Kennington sitting around eating those chickens, laughing and drinking whiskey. It is tragic how blind we humans can be to our fate. For some that night, the chickens would be one of their last meals. Perhaps it was good to be blind to what the future held for us; otherwise, we may never have enjoyed one last good laugh together. If we were able to see our own tragic death before it happened—who could ever smile?

Tom Ziehm and Doc MacSwan

Like A Sunday Walk

February, 1968:

After the Can Tho mission and the construction of a new firebase, we were flown back to Dong Tam. My platoon had a three day stand-down, giving us a chance to write letters, watch movies, play volleyball, smoke grass and stock up on necessities from the PX. Once the exhaustion from the mission was slept off, we spent our nights at the enlisted club playing poker, a beer or cigarette in one hand, our cards in the other. We complained about everything under the sun, exchanging insults for conversation with comments like—"Dam your ugly" or "I bet your wife is sucking dick right about now." Most of us were stoned. Smoking marijuana was like drinking beer—nobody thought anything of it.

Ting had become an excellent poker player. When he first arrived at the 2nd Platoon, Ting was quiet, but after long hours at the card table and fighting in combat for his life, he was one of us. He was very likable, always smiled, loved Americans and was tough as nails. While playing cards with Ting I could never tell if he was bluffing; he always had a shit-eating grin on his face, whether his cards were good or bad. He was short and thin, with wiry muscles and had saved our asses many times out in the bush. He lived in a small, heavily guarded village outside Dong Tam with his wife, children and grandmother. If the opportunity presented itself, the Viet Cong would have gone to great lengths to kill Ting and his family—or any Vietnamese in the Chieu Hoi program.

Although Ting and I had become close, my tightest friendship remained with Tom Ziehm. We drank ourselves drunk many nights, hugging, laughing, cursing and singing with Bruce Johnson, Roy Moseman and Billy Kennington right beside us. My friendship with Tom was much deeper than the bottle, having formed an intimate relationship of shared thoughts and concerns. Significant conversations were saved for in the barracks or late at night in the jungle while conversations at the enlisted club were loud, with little depth.

In the barracks we separated into our close knit circles. Tom, Bruce, Roy, Billy and I shot the shit on the bunks, reading personal letters to eachother. Billy Kennington often asked us to proof read letters home to his wife. Sanky Thomas, Richardson and Washington formed a circle of black guys. Sgt.

Williams and Freeman were close, sometimes keeping to themselves late at night. Before the night was over, the friendship circles broke up a bit. The marijuana smokers went outside to smoke a joint and the men that liked to take pain pills got up from their bunks to get a drink of water. When it was time to hit the rack, thoughts of home came with the touch of the pillow. First my eyes were wide, staring through the blackness, seeing the faces of my loved ones, then my eyes closed and the faces of loved ones remained. A hard night of drinking and smoking grass is often what I needed to sleep.

We stayed in Dong Tam after the stand-down, during which time Sgt. Williams broke the news we had to pull an Area of Operation (AO) mission around Dong Tam, which lasted between one and three days.

Our platoon formed up by squad outside the barracks. The morning was beautiful, not a cloud in the sky. Everyone scrambled to check their gear, making sure nothing was forgotten. I looked inside my aid bag with a quick glance, hoping I wouldn't have to use the morphine or cravat bandages. With the all too familiar words, Sgt. Williams yelled out, "Saddle up...Lock and load." The guards at the entrance, knowing of our mission, opened the concertina wire gate, letting our two columns of infantrymen out and into "no man's land."

The first field we crossed was a wasteland of dry, cracked earth with small pockets of yellow grass withered under the scorch of the sun. We headed for a distant jungle, vibrant and green, yet stained with the blood of American and Viet Cong soldiers. We pressed on crossing several drainage ditches, sinking into mud and water up to our knees, smacking at mosquitoes and wiping sweat from our eyes. We broke for lunch and began the typical complaining, bitching about the water in our boots, the stench of the mud and swelling insect bites. Our guns were never more than a short reach away. We took turns talking about home or bitching about the Nam, seemingly relaxed, leaning against trees in semi-circles, heating up coffee, trading foods and smoking cigarettes.

After lunch we moved slowly, entering the village of Andook, where a little girl was burning up with a fever. Greeted by her mother, I walked into the hooch and knelt beside the girl lying on a bamboo mat covered with a colorful blanket. I took her temperature; it was high but not critical enough for her to need I.V. fluids from the hospital. With my canteen of water in hand, I placed an aspirin in her mouth, gave her a smile of comfort and wiped the sweat from her face. I knew outside the hooch the GI's handed out candy to a crowd of children, so on my way out I gave some chocolate to the mother for when her daughter felt better.

I left the hooch, stepping into the light of sun and a cloudless sky. Old feeble men sat on the ground, leaning against hooches, high on opium, trying to kill the painful trauma done to their bodies after a lifetime of farming. The villages all seemed to be the same—they were ancient, untouched by time, changed only by the horrors of war.

The threat of the enemy seemed distant under the rumble of Dong Tam. We left the village on a small dirt path surrounded by jungle. In pockets, the sun shined through a narrow gap in the canopy of jungle, sending streams of light to the ground in the center of the path. Like a lion lurking in the shade, we avoided the light, keeping to the sides of our passageway. The day was calm and the humidity low, like being on a Sunday walk. Tuning out the distant rumble of Dong Tam, I listened to the chirp of the birds echoing all around me. Faintly breaking the silence, Lt. Dimagard and Sgt. Williams whispered plans about where to set up for the night.

The sun began to set as our leaders, Lt. Dimagard, Sgt. Williams and Sgt. Maynard decided where to place our ambush for the night, giving us a large open field to our rear toward Dong Tam with the 1st and 3rd within a couple kilometers on each flank. Our nerves weren't on edge with all of our firepower pointed at one tree line 100 feet away. After breaking up in squads and forming a small perimeter around the Command Post, we ate dinner with watchful eyes.

Saturated socks and boots were placed in the remaining sunlight. Before putting on dry socks, everyone put on anti-fungal cream to combat the constant foot saturation of water. The wet terrain of the Mekong Delta inflicted several men, but it was Tom with the most severe case of jungle rot. Although Tom's skin may have been more susceptible to fungus; his calmness under fire, more often than not, placed him at the point of our platoon. That position left him more waterlogged than most as he repeatedly waded into water of unknown depth, only to climb out and say, "Don't wanna cross here." And it was those trouble spots in the Delta where the Viet Cong liked to hit us, in deep canals with our guns held over our heads like a wolverine without claws. But where we rested that night, felt as good as it would get.

The night cascaded across the jungle and waving green grass fields. Our voices lowered to a whisper. Tom's 1st squad was out on the perimeter and he radioed us that he was moving slowly toward our Command Post. When Tom slipped in, he crawled under a poncho with Sgt. Williams and Maynard, looking at a map with a red lens flashlight, going over the next day's movement. Beside me, Overcast was writing a letter, his heavy radio unit propped on a tree between us. Lt. Dimagard closed his eyes after finishing a talk with me about running track in high school; he was a long distance mile runner, and I was a quarter mile runner. While others slept, we took turns working the radio, contacting the squads out on perimeter. Although it was dark with ominous shadows, our

Sunday walk ended with a moonlit, star-studded sky.

Sgt. Wilborn, a light skinned black man with a slow southern accent, found himself sitting on our perimeter that night. I wasn't acquainted with him, but knew that he had a wife waiting for him back home. Gerald Elfman, a very likable guy, was also there that night. He was short, with no defining features about his face. His plump face sometimes hid even his smile. Elfman was one of the few GI's in the platoon that wasn't skinny from walking in the Nam, but I don't think he had been there very long.

I slept in the CP that night next to Lt. Dimagard, Overcast, Maynard, and Sgt. Williams. We talked about home, favorite foods, women, wives and sports heroes. In the field, Dimagard talked to us like one of the guys, as equals, yet made it clear he was the head honcho. We slept with our dreams—if sleep is what you would call it. Sleeping in the jungle was more of a careful balance between consciousness and unconsciousness. In complete exhaustion, it seemed the moment I closed my eyes the morning light came instantly.

The Sunday walk continued into the next day. With the sun hanging high and bright, we broke for lunch, eating everything from peaches and pound cake to canned ham mixed with lima beans to name a few. We saddled up and moved out, stomachs full, finishing up cigarettes and chasing the smoke with

Chicklet gum. Sgt. Wilborn's squad took point for the platoon, almost immediately finding signs that an enemy mortar team had been there, foot printing several areas with flattened grass like a giant deer bed. While walking, my mind often wandered with thoughts of home, but the reality of war quickly brought my thoughts back to the mission.

Sgt. Wilborn's lead squad moved off the path, cut through a small ditch and stepped up on a mounded dike that crossed through a large expanse of muddy rice paddies. Although dikes were often chosen by the Viet Cong for the placement of booby traps, we took our chances with the dry ground rather than walking in knee high mud.

Beyond the fields was jungle, the sun, and chirping birds, all radiating in their own way. The point squad walked painfully slow across the fields. In a second the calmness was shattered, birds flew from their perches as the sunlight shining on Sgt. Wilborn was shrouded in a cloud of explosive dust when a booby trap was tripped. The earth shook, sending adrenaline through my veins. The word "Medic" shrieked through the air, but I was already on my way, running to Sgt. Wilborn, sinking in mud, gun in one hand and my aid bag in the other. The platoon formed a line perimeter along both sides of the dike, waiting for an all out ambush. The air became ghostly silent, except for the moans of the wounded.

At Sgt. Wilborn's side I kneeled down, his eyes wide, mouth wide open, he let out the sounds of his anguish and pain. I began assessing his wounds, feeling his pulse, checking his eyes and cutting the remainder of shredded clothing from his legs. His testicles were hanging out of their sacks in a bloody mess, filled with shrapnel and covered in mud. With a torturous pain in his groin, I quickly gave him morphine and watched his body grow limp. His eyes filled with tears of fear, pain, sadness and anger all in one. It looked like inside he was saying, "Why me?" I told him "Don't move... you gotta lay still... it's not pretty but I'm gonna get ya the fuck out of here."

I instructed Tom and Wilbanks to lift his tattered legs in the air as Sgt. Williams gave comfort holding his head. As they lifted Sgt. Wilborn's legs, I wrapped a cravat diaper around his waist, placed wet gauze on his testicles, then cinched it up. I comforted him with my hand on his shoulder and looked into his tearful eyes, filled with horror and question.

The Dustoff helicopter was incoming and I radioed the nature of the wounds to the medic inside the approaching chopper as Sgt. Williams, with a handful of men, secured a Landing Zone in the rice field next to the dike. We popped a purple haze smoke grenade to indicate the evacuation point and the helicopter quickly moved to our position. Sgt. Wilborn lay on a stretcher carried by Wilbanks,

Tom and me. Sgt. Williams walked beside us still trying to give comfort to our wounded brother. We loaded him into the helicopter, slapping him on the shoulder, telling him he was a lucky mother fucker, doing our best to say good-bye.

I watched him lift into the sky with a shitty feeling inside. The other men became quiet, realizing it could have been them. I looked at my hands and noticing the human tissue and blood on my skin, knelt down with my canteen in hand to wash off the waste. The guys left me alone, giving me some space, but I don't think I needed the space. It wasn't going to change a damn thing. The eyes of a wounded man said so much, they'd peer through me with a thousand emotions and questions for God. The eyes of the wounded left me feeling nauseated and helpless, like their turmoil radiated through me. But more than anything I felt the eyes glaring at me to be their savior, leaving me feeling alone, trying to feverishly treat wounds that were untreatable. We moved out shortly after, like nothing ever happened, but our minds were filled with the wounds sustained by Wilborn's body.

Thinking of Sgt. Wilborn, unable to completely block out the horror, made sleeping difficult that night. Death and suffering was still fairly new to me. Sgt. Williams on the other hand had seen it all before, but he was also quiet after a man was killed or wounded, usually muttering something like, "Cock suckers." That second night went by uneventful; however, the lion was still hiding in the grass. The night was clear and the stars could be seen, as we held tight to our dreams of home. It was like we were gripping something with all the might in our hands, fighting an unyielding force that was trying to smash and wrench our grip of longing to be home. If the constant grasping for our dreams of home were given up, perhaps sanity would go with it.

Happy Birthday

March, 1968:

AO missions were taking a bloody toll on us. We'd blow a booby trap, take a cigarette break, move on further, spot another, set more C-4 charges and blow that one. Covered in mud and stinking like the land itself, we relentlessly searched for traps. That was the ideal mission, but too often, the booby traps were detonated by the foot of one of our men. AO missions were more frustrating than firefights. At least in a firefight we had the opportunity to fight back, but booby traps left no outlet for our frustration, leaving us with no clear victory. I woke up each day knowing we would lose more men in the Mekong Delta, but could only hope my number wasn't up yet.

Everyone loved Ting. I couldn't count how many times he saved one of us from tripping a booby trap. It was strange knowing several years before I met Ting, when he was a Viet Cong Lieutenant, he was the one setting traps against the

Americans. He knew where and how the enemy placed them and when he spotted one, he didn't rush up to it—he knew the Viet Cong would sometimes make one trap visible and a second trap more concealed. Ting's expertise was irreplaceable, but sadly, it was not always enough.

Once nightfall had come, our perimeter was established and inside the CP we continued talks about home. Lt. Dimagard often reminisced over some girl from college and his business plans in South America after Vietnam. He had a good sense of humor, which was not always the case for a platoon leader. I could tell he was extremely intelligent, but he talked to us and not over us. In him, the only conceit detected was his ability as a leader and that's just what we wanted—to be lead by a man of confidence. On July 7, 1967, five months before he arrived in Vietnam, he wrote a letter to his parents while he was training in Georgia. He said:

> Dear Mom and Dad,
> I'm brigade staff duty officer tonight. All it means is sitting around all night making sure nobody steals the headquarters building. Nobody has tried yet and I'm not expecting any action along those lines.
>
> I'm really getting sick of this place. I'm a training officer who never has any time to train men. The whole day is inevitably spent doing

paperwork explaining how the men are getting trained, which they never get because everybody is too busy talking about it.

Anyway, orders to Vietnam at this stage would be considered a blessing. The way things have been going for the other men, I should get a warning order shortly. The warning order usually gives a two-month notice. After a 30-day leave I'd be heading over.

Our new quarters are really a dream. They are extremely comfortable in all respects. One thing about Georgia: the bugs by variety and numbers are a real problem, they're everywhere. I remember how I had to hunt for those 25 different kinds of bugs for the high school biology class. Around here you just open the door and you get at least 25.

Let me tell you about my roommates. I lucked out getting such good ones considering the way I had to scrounge them. Jeff Kucklick is an Army brat who originates from South Carolina. He's been all over the world and done just about everything in the process. He's the type that's crazy about mechanical things. He's always got some kind of an off—the—wall project going. If something doesn't work, he'll fix it (or at least take it apart). Bill Townsend is a real good-natured guy of 20 who comes from Pittsburgh. He hasn't been around too much and is still impressed by how much beer he can drink. He's a nice guy to have around, though.

To kill the time I read a lot of Army manuals. I'm trying to keep up on things for Nam. (It's a wise man who'll work a couple of years to live another 50.) When I get sick of that I plan my trip for South America. I may never take that thing but I'm having a lot of fun planning for it. From what I've read things are really wide open down there. It'd be a good area of consideration if I decide to get into international commerce.

I've started dating a girl from Atlanta. Don't ask: "Why Atlanta?" It's because there isn't a darn thing in this town for a guy who isn't interested in married women. And I'm not. Out of the 20 NCO's in our company, there have been 3 divorces since I've been here. That's pretty bad news.

I'm going to grab some rack time.
Love
Bill

March 8, 1968:

It was my wife's birthday and my platoon was back on an AO mission around Dong Tam. Waking up at dawn, we twisted and bent the discomfort out of our bodies. I pulled out my P-38 can opener and some C-Rations. Wilbanks sat beside me, sitting behind his machine gun, the barrel peaking out of the brush, aimed down a narrow path. We ate different meals: beefsteak, chopped ham and eggs and turkey loaf. Our greatest luxury was a strong cup of instant coffee. As always, we used small pieces of C-4 high explosive, rather than heat tabs for heating up coffee and nearly all of our cooking. Back at the base camp, supply would ask where all the C-4 was going. They'd say, "Been blowing a lot of bunkers?" I would reply, "Ya...all over the place...beaucoup...beaucoup." Inside I would be laughing, thinking about the stockpile of heat tabs everyone had.

Slowly dragging around Overcast by the radio unit on his back, Lt. Dimagard paced, talking with the company commander, coordinating movements for the day. Sgt. Williams notified Tom his 2nd squad was on point and the time to move out was at hand. Final sips of coffee, peach juice and cigarette drags were completed. Tom checked his gear and took a look around, assuring himself he wasn't going alone, only first. Facing his squad of men he said, "2nd squad...saddle-up...on me." After a brief moment, he stepped out of the jungle, onto the path and into the unknown.

Our platoon began to lengthen into a staggered column, avoiding the sunlight by holding tight to the sides of the path. Eyes cautiously searched the ground before each step. It was my turn to head out. Sgt. Williams designated one of the squads for rear guard, which at times could be just as dangerous as the point. Once Sgt. Williams joined the column, I did too along with Lt. Dimagard and Overcast. There was really no safe haven in the platoon, even the middle of the platoon seemed safe, but the Viet Cong also knew the command and control wouldn't be at the front or rear. Of course Overcast's radio unit, with its 25-foot antenna, made Dimagard stick out like a sore thumb anyways.

While moving, Sgt. Williams and Sgt. Maynard slowly made their way through the length of the platoon. When the terrain changed, moving from jungle to field or field to jungle, or crossing a water filled ditch, Williams and Dimagard would converse with Ting about the area, knowing the Mekong was his backyard. We passed by several farmers working in the rice fields, conscious to the fact that any one of them could have been a Viet Cong guerrilla.

The morning sun was high, without a single cloud masking its heat, the humidity strangely low. The entire morning was spent following the dirt path, finding no sign of enemy tracks. Moving on the path and in the sun allowed pants to dry, but always wet were our feet—if not from water, they were soaked with sweat. As noon approached, Lt.

Dimagard began slowing the pace, stopping often, searching for a secure spot.

Shaded with palms and banana trees, dense with jungle, the ancient path we walked cut through two enormous rice fields. The lack of cover left me feeling vulnerable, like I was being watched. I looked at Tom's eyes and without words, knew he was feeling the same uneasiness. We broke for lunch on the edge of a jungle. Wilbanks was at the rear of the platoon with the 2nd squad, his heavy machine gun pointing down our back trail. The bitching and complaining started with the opening of C-Rations, the peaches were too crispy for fruit—like hardened jelly, and the fruitcake was like a rock. GI's would say, "If the gun jams with mud, then hit 'em in the head with fruit cake." The funny thing is we all knew, if it came down to it, to save our own life, we'd pick up that fruitcake.

Some of the men were heating water inside their helmets or (pots), which heated enough water for several GI's. Under a nice shade tree I found comfort and leaned against the towering palm, setting up my own cooking area. Tom and Moose, bitching about being on point, came and sat down beside me, soaked in mud with wet feet, Tom's were covered with the fungus of jungle rot. With helmets sitting low over their eyes, the most prevalent sight was the rubber Superman figures in the front of Tom and Moose's helmets. I started bitching at him, "Get them fucking boots off

Ziehm." Tom replied with a wisp of air, "Ya...ya...ya." The jungle rot was pestering Tom, forcing him to put dry socks on several times throughout the day. I pulled out an extra pair of socks from my aid bag and threw them at his chest.

Roy Moseman with his good old boy state of Georgia sense of humor, sat down beside us along with Billy Don Kennington. Over the sound of all the shit talk, was the distant thumping of 155 Howitzer cannons in Dong Tam, a couple of klicks (kilometers) away. Lt. Dimagard was back on the radio with command, finding out where the enemy was spotted and plotting our next movement.

After moving all day without incident, it was late and a night position had to be found and secured before sunset. Sgt. Williams went forward with a squad of men to search an area while the rest of us waited for their return with chocolate or a cigarette in hand. About fifteen minutes passed when Sgt. Williams returned, informing Lt. Dimagard there was an island of jungle in the middle of a rice paddy. We saddled up and moved toward the island. Gerald Elfman, with his friendly round face and Scotty, a red haired boy from Oklahoma walked in front of me with the sun at our backs.

Our quiet pace was shattered again fleeing all previous thought. I felt the sting of shrapnel hit my left side. I was hit, but through the falling cloud of dust and debris, I saw Elfman squirming on the ground in pain and Scotty sitting up holding a disfigured arm. Forgetting about the wounds on my left arm and shoulder, I went to Elfman first and cut off his pant legs. His left side was hit badly. There was little blood, mostly oozing body fluid and small pieces of rusty steel slivered inside the flesh covering his hip and upper thigh. After making sure no shrapnel hit any vitals, I gave him morphine then strapped a wet gauze pad on his side and secured it.

I looked in his tormented eyes with a comforting gesture and said, "Your OK man… your gonna be with the nurses for awhile." I turned my attention to Scotty, holding a disfigured arm. The shrapnel hit his arm with such force his bones ripped through the skin and overlapped each other. His arm was so disfigured it was difficult for me to splint. Although Scotty's arm bone was horribly snapped in half, he didn't give a fuck; he was going home. His pain was less than the joy of going home and when I wrapped his arm, he had a smile on his face, cursing and swearing over the pain, but happy as a mother fucker.

Scotty sat on the ground holding his arm and I began to feel my own shrapnel wounds start to ache. The muscles in my left arm began to stiffen, making it difficult to bend my elbow. When the Dustoff helicopter touched down we said our goodbyes and Tom, Moose and I loaded Gerald Elfman into the chopper on his good side. I looked into him with a hidden sadness and he looked into me with thanks, but not a word was said. The Huey lifted into the air holding the two wounded men. I can still taste the churning, purple-hazed dust and feel its grit in my eyes. I felt empty of everything but emotion and wonder. Scotty sat close to the door of the chopper, his good arm holding a motionless wave of good-bye, with the familiar love/hate look on his face— love your brothers, hate the Nam.

I walked back to Dong Tam with the rest of the platoon, my arm and shoulder stiff with pain. Back at base, medical personal picked the shrapnel out with tweezers with the help of a magnet they placed over the punctures. For one week I was placed on a medical stand down, having my wounds examined every day for infection. In base camp I lost the madness of the Nam the best I could, with the help of beer and marijuana. Sometimes I drank and smoked inside the barracks and other times, I went to the gun bunker, where we drank, smoked and listened to music. I embraced the boredom with a cigarette in one hand, a beer in the other. I was unaware that my youth was beginning to fade, my innocence gone. The perception of life and the way that I saw it was being changed forever.

Constantly the combat soldier is being changed—being desensitized to the horror around them. Tom Ziehm and Moose Johnson, the other super troopers, were being changed as well. All of us were carried away by evil times, changing us for an eternity. Lt. Dimagard carried the burden of holding in emotion and looking strong for his men; yet his inner soul was being transformed. Sgt. Williams was already hardened by the death and mutilation of humans. There were no more Sunday walks. The security felt around Dong Tam was gone forever.

On patrol Gerald Elfman, Sergeant Williams and Doc MacSwan.

Unspoken Thoughts

March, 1968:

The 4th of the 47th was placed back on riverine operations and the Tango boats picked us up in the Dong Tam harbor. We were dropped off on a barge beside the USS Colleton and walked up a steep flight of stairs and into the ship. The air-conditioning and Navy food were my greatest luxuries. I settled into my new home, personalizing it with a picture of my wife over my pillow and favorite letters sprayed with her perfume hung from the ceiling. Everyone did it, surrounding themselves with ornaments from home, some men even slept with favorite photographs.

Like most missions we boarded the Tango boats before daylight. I wasn't sure where we were going, but I knew the mission was going to be a long one, deep into the heart of the jungle for several days. Our convoy with an enormous amount of firepower traveled the large waters of the Song My Tho River for an hour and turned, idling our way single file through a narrow canal for several hours, the shoreline only a few feet away from the sides of the boat.

We unloaded near a village with no resistance. Upon entering, I noticed a small stream running through the center of the village, the water brown, shallow and smelling of raw sewage. The villagers looked different from the Vietnamese near Dong Tam; their facial features were narrow and their eyes more wide and oval. Because we had traveled such a great distance to the village, Tom and I thought we were near Cambodia, but we really didn't know.

It was clear the Viet Cong were using the small village, leaving behind enough rice to feed a large army of about a thousand men. It struck enough fear in me to start glassing the distant jungle. It was a different kind of landscape. Unlike the marshy, flat plains of the delta, the distant jungle was heavy on sloping hills with hard, tree-rooted soil. The hills revealed the vastness of the land, stretching as far as the horizon whereas the rice fields revealed only the tree line in front of us. Before I came to the village, I thought how much nicer it was than walking up to my waist in water and to my knees in mud.

With weapons to our shoulders, we immediately began searching the homes and asking for identification. Leading a search into one of the hooches was a new Sergeant who had replaced Sgt. Wilborn. The floor was mud and the bamboo shutters covering the windows were open around the entire hooch, revealing other hooches along the muddy stream. A woman was inside by herself acting nervous and Ting began talking to her, interpreting her words back to our sergeant at a rapid pace.

One of us found a hidden bunker underneath a steel plate covered over with earth. Lifting the plate cautiously with guns drawn and eyes wide, we heard movement inside the hole. Seconds after the noise, through an open window we saw a young man running toward the stream, escaping from a secondary exit underneath the hooch. The new sergeant to our platoon stormed out in a full run, catching the skinny, young Vietnamese man just before the stream. The sergeant struggled to hold him, but the Vietnamese man scratched him with his finger nails on the face and without another thought punched him in the head, knocking him to the ground. From the shock of the punch, the sergeant's watch from his wife busted loose and landed in the stream. He looked in the water for several seconds, but soon realized his search through the thick filthy water was in vain.

Looking back at the Vietnamese man, rage was in his eyes and his face held no expression. The sergeant pulled out his .45 caliber pistol and shot the young man in the chest, blowing him back into the stream where the brown water began to turn red. Immediately, the mother jumped into the water, screaming with tears, holding her dead son, trying to revive him. The mother frantically tried pulling her son out of the water, but after a few second of shock and watching her weak body struggle to pull her dead son from the water, we pulled the body for her. The mother knelt on the water's edge over her lifeless child; her weeping echoed through the small village.

I remember that day clearly in my mind, a day of profound awakening. Inside the command post that night we talked briefly about the facts of the shooting. Lieutenant Dimagard didn't say too much after his briefing, but we all knew that the sergeant was in a boat load of shit with command in the most serious degree.

I had a conscious thought with Tom—I had just seen a young man shot to death over a watch and deep inside my inner most being, I felt more sadness for the sergeant losing his watch than the loss of a young man's life. I thought, "Oh my God, I am not the same."

In the morning we left the village, leaving nothing behind for the Viet Cong. On the way back to the flotilla, I was consumed in thought. My eyes were opened and for the first time I looked into the window of my soul, finding it hardened to the emotional pain of others and unsympathetic to cruelty.

The next riverine operation came quickly. We spent most of the morning struggling through thick mud and water and finally came to a canal with a narrow crossing bridge made of bamboo. The Vietnamese formed the bridge by tying two bamboo poles together in an x-shape, laying several of these structures across the canal, tying them all together with more bamboo across all the centers, thereby creating a narrow walk way. Several men had already crossed and then I carefully walked the center of the bridge, paying close attention to the setting of each step.

As the new sergeant that killed the young Vietnamese man began moving across the bridge he slipped. His body flipped up over the bamboo handrail, but rather than falling into the water, he grabbed a bamboo pole and swung his body toward the narrow walkway. His body whipped around while he held on with one arm, impaling himself onto the bamboo x-structure, puncturing his groin just below his testicles. He screamed in pain with several inches of the bamboo still inside him. I quickly came to his side and started assessing his injury while he cursed out loud, "Get me off this fucking thing." As much as I wanted to get the bamboo out of his groin, I knew pulling it out could cause severe bleeding if any arteries were hit.

Several men jumped into the canal and lifted him in the air, taking some of the weight off the bamboo inside him. Sgt. Williams held the bamboo several inches away from the entry point as I cut through it with a saw, his screams intensified as the bamboo moved with each hack of my saw. When I finished cutting, we carried him through the water, rested him on the shore and waited for the Dustoff to come in. I gave him morphine for the pain and put a girdle around him. He rested on his back, his pelvis shifted upward, keeping the several inches of protruding bamboo off the ground.

While waiting for the helicopter I looked at several other men including Tom, all of us with the same startled look of "I wonder?" Not a single word was said, but my eyes and thoughts focused on the clouds above. I thought, "Could it be, in this hell of a place, God is still in control?" Although I only talked to Tom about it, I'm sure that everyone who saw the shooting thought the same thing.

Again I realized the Nam was changing me—as if the war itself was preparing my mind for future events. I no longer felt in control and in a strange way, when I was cutting the bamboo trying to free the sergeant, I felt an enormous presence of God. It confused me as much as it gave me clarity. Maybe it was just the moment—nothing more, nothing less. But Tom and I were not the only ones to feel it. Nobody said anything about God's wrath and right and wrong—we were all riding the fence on that. Even if we didn't commit a cruel act of vengeance, few could say they were innocent of the thought.

The combat soldier is filled with unspoken words—an entire language of our own. We didn't talk about the dead and wounded or about good and evil. In our minds we were in hell already.

Goodness was simply being alive or in one piece and evil was just war itself. Anger, sadness, fear and question were all part of our unspoken language, a language easily understood, pouring from our eyes, not our mouths. We were all filled with the same suffering, witnessing the atrocities of war, making the unspoken words recognizable.

On the way back to the flotilla of the Riverine Force nothing was said again about the sergeant, nor do I know if he was ever investigated. Future combat missions would soon flee the ponderings I had on that day. When we returned to the ship reeking of the Mekong itself and unloaded the troop carriers, we were hosed down on the barge like animals, standing in pools of mud, our feet shriveled, legs aching with fatigue. I hit the air conditioning and it felt like a weight had been lifted off of me. We talked about home, favorite foods, cars and girls, and we drank our allotted two beers. With the help of Budweiser sleep soon followed.

The Orphanage

The USS Colleton was a giant refrigerator of air conditioning. We loved it, but being on the ship also meant more search and destroy missions. We played cards just like in Dong Tam. After six weeks on airmobile, the move to the ships was a change that served as a milestone—one move closer to home. For Kennington, sitting in the cool confines of the boat, it was one more milestone toward seeing his son again and for me, transferring to the ships was one more toward seeing my wife again. Everyone had something to return to—for some it was a city block with a bunch of buddies, sipping on cold beer in the hot sun, listening to Motown. For others, it was hunting with their father or smoothing up on a high school sweetheart. But before that could happen many rice fields and jungles had to be crossed and muddy water-filled ditches had to be waded.

That evening Sgt. Williams came in and said, "Sweet dreams boys...Tango boats b-wait'n...0500." We all knew what that meant—the next few days would be spent walking in mud, standing in water up to our waists and fighting off mosquitoes. I knew it also meant possibly not returning home alive. With these thoughts, we slept soundly in the air conditioned quarters, dreaming of home.

The next morning on the ship, we ate the finest chow available in Vietnam. After grabbing our gear we swiftly headed down the stairs to the barge. In the water the diesel engines rumbled, misting the air with fumes. My company formed up on the barge consumed with fear and wonder. A few minutes after loading into the Tango boats and taking our seats, the engines roared in reverse and pulled off the pontoons, putting the dim red lights behind us. The radio chatter could barely be heard over the engines and few words were said. The faces around me said more than a mouthful—faces without emotion, radiated anxiety.

Surrounding the entire convoy was a thick cloud of diesel fumes. A slight breeze sometimes brought the fumes into the troop bay, but none of us thought anything of it. Everyone was quiet, without a smile, each of us preparing for the mission ahead of us in our own way. The closer we came to the Landing Zone, the thicker the sense of fear became. I read my white Bible and others formed the sign of the cross over their chest or held rosaries in their hands. It was all the same, just different ways of preparing for the brutality and horror of combat.

We had seen fierce resistance during the Tet Offensive, but persevered through it with victory.

Most of the NVA and Viet Cong forces were decimated and disbanded, but the threat of the enemy was still very real for us. As more time elapsed since the main offensive of Tet, the enemy increased its unification and organization in the Delta region. Small, but violent, firefights were increasing with the reorganization of enemy units.

Outside the boat I could hear the Landing Zone getting prepped with F-4 phantom jets and artillery shells screeching through the air. It was a small sense of comfort knowing an area had been saturated with high explosives and Napalm before we moved in. The Viet Cong often waited out the massive bombardments in tunnels, only to climb back out of their holes and set up ambushes for the approaching infantry.

The boat began to turn into the shore for landing. Sgt. Williams had everyone up, giving a quick gear check. On both sides of me a Navy gunner gripped his M-50 machine gun. I listened intently to the lowered idle of the boat's engines. I knew our landing was imminent and I hoped the 20mm cannon over my head stayed quiet. My landing craft neared the shore along with the other Tango boats. The Monitor and Alpha boats covered us with a massive arsenal of big guns and mortars.

Taking a deep breath I said one last prayer. I felt the earth sliding against the hull of the boat; the landing only seconds away. The ramp lowered and I dashed off the boat with the rest of my platoon.

Two other Tango boats unloaded on the same shore beside us and behind us, the Monitor and Alpha boats continued to guard us, just as a lion watches over its pride.

I half stood in knee high grass beside Lt. Dimagard and could hear him on the radio with the company commander discerning the approach into the village. We quickly formed a straight-line perimeter along the canal and waited for the command to move out. In the distance F-4 Phantom jets continued to shriek the air, shaking the earth with their ordinance, leaving elongated plumes of napalm to dominate the distant landscape. Sgt. Williams made the call, "2nd squad…you got point!"

I fell in behind the lead squad, forced my eyes off the distant carnage and began scanning the immediate area for the enemy. The destruction ahead of me became clearer with each step that I took. Several clouds of smoke ascended from the village and the surrounding area and a rotten egg smell was in the air from the explosives. High in the sky, two Huey Cobras circled the vicinity waiting for an enemy target,

The village was upon us and the smell of rotten eggs was then mixed with the scent of death. Before we entered the village our platoon broke into squads, two of which flanked outside the village. I followed the 2nd into the village, bringing the stench of death even nearer. The jungle behind the small hamlet was a raging inferno, cracking and popping as the fire burned out of control. Smoke swirled in the wind and across the images of women and children that wept on their knees in the dirt, holding dead loved ones, beating their chests and pounding the ground with their hands. I noticed several structures were decimated to nothing but smoldering ashes.

Ting had begun to interpret the villager's cry and was the first to know of the horrific tragedy. We came to find out one of our artillery rounds fell short, landing on a school house and an orphanage. We quickly moved to the sight of the disaster and found the remains of a scorched wooden building with steel sheets of roofing littered on the ground. Piled up four feet high like sandbags, I looked with sickness at dead babies and children, noticing many of them had blond hair—orphaned by American men.

The sight and smell of death overwhelmed my senses and I felt like I was crying, yet no tears fell from my eyes. I focused through the smoky air and cutting through me like a double edged sword, my eye's looked into those of a little girl holding a headless doll, gripping it tightly as if the doll was the most precious thing on earth. Her glare filled me with such contrition I was forced to look away from her, like God himself was telling me, "You are not worthy to look upon such innocence."

We continued through the village, surrounded by the screams and stench of war. When we left, women grabbed dirt and threw it at me, while others spit from their mouth. I will never forget the raw feelings inside my soul, feelings of helplessness, disgust and anger. I hated war, but as an infantryman, the only way to live was to fight.

After leaving the village we moved through a desolate landscape of destruction. The area was so destroyed and burned it resembled the surface of the moon, with bomb craters and the absence of all green. Everything was ash in color and smelled like rotten eggs. The feeling of death overpowered the land and I felt empty inside.

My mind has blocked out much of the blood and gore I witnessed, but never the sight of that little girl. The image came back to me over the years; it was, and still is to this day, a constant reminder of the dreadfulness of war. Many people have tried to describe the sufferings in war, but it's pretty simple—war just fucking sucks.

Just Another Day

March 19, 1968:

Within a mile of Dong Tam the Tango boats dropped us off on the west bank of the Route 66 canal to execute another monotonous, but deadly, search and destroy operation. Stepping off the boat, the shoreline was dry, mounded high above a large rice field that was flooded with muddy water. Several dikes crossed the field's length and with the enemy knowing we would walk the dry dikes, rather than sloshing through knee deep water and mud, the odds were that some of the narrow earthen mounds were booby trapped.

The assault boats rested in the water as we descended to the rice field from the shoreline of the canal. Slowly, we closed the distance between us and a dark haunting jungle that stood like a black iron curtain several hundred yards away. My dry feet were sucked into the wet muck, making each step a tiresome chore of pulling and twisting my boots from the quagmire of mud. Lt. Dimagard and Overcast were in front of me, Overcast carrying the radio pack with its 25 foot whip antenna seemed to be an obvious target for an enemy sniper to take a crack at killing or wounding our commander and radio operator. I continued on with my trudge through the sloppy mud and with thoughts of home, I tried ignoring the aching in my legs. The closer we moved toward the jungle, the more intense I felt we were being watched. It was as if the jungle itself was alive with peering eyes, studying our every move, plotting and conspiring to attack us.

After an hour of grinding through the mud, my legs became numb to the punishment. It was a similar sensation to one I had while running the mile for the track team in high school. The first quarter mile was grueling, but my legs soon took on a life of there own, separated from the thoughts of my mind. At some point, all of our minds had to accept the physical pain and exhaustion of walking through the Mekong Delta.

My legs continued to move on their own and my mind drifted into remembrances of my wife—the drive-ins we went to, watching very little of the movie, kissing and hugging with a brief glance at the giant screen. And also the many walks on my in-laws farm, where we made love in the wheat fields. There were hundreds of memories I could draw upon, taking my mind off the exhaustion, but they always simmered down to the harsh reality that I was in Vietnam.

The struggled walk began to end as Tom, up on point, stepped out of the rice field and onto a dike. I moved closer to the dry ground, watching one by one, each man ahead of me, stepping up and out of the flooded field, legs covered in the decaying stench of the delta. Then, from the sweltering heat of the sun, as quickly as we stepped out of the water and onto the dry dike, the mud almost instantly dried on our pant legs with a musty reek.

In the front of the platoon, Tom moved at a snail's pace, finally bringing us to within a hundred yards of the menacing jungle. As we moved closer, each of my steps were nearly frozen with fear. Lt. Dimagard brought us to a halt and called on the radio for a marking round over the jungle. Seconds later, over our heads, I heard the whistle of the artillery shell and followed the noise through the air, then watched it burst into a puff of red smoke over the jungle in front of us. We knew then, if we were ambushed, within seconds the artillery unit in Dong Tam could decimate the enemy after their initial burst of fire which is why the Viet Cong usually fled the area after ambushing us with a brief, but high volume of fire leaving us nothing to shoot at.

We converged on the tree line. My breath was heavy with fear and the seconds seemed like hours. I couldn't help but remember, barely two weeks prior to that day, the 1st Platoon getting cut to pieces, trapped like fish in a barrel, desperately trying to crawl from the field, seeking shelter in the jungle. I stood as a helpless medic watching it all. I also reminded myself what Sgt. Williams told me after he tackled me to the ground, "You ain't worth shit to me dead, Doc," his voice shockingly calm under a hail of gunfire. When Sgt. Williams told me that his eyes scared me and penetrated through me the truth—the truth that I didn't know shit about Vietnam.

Finally, the torturous walk ended when Tom reached the jungle and knelt down. Our entire platoon froze in its tracks, listening and searching with wide eyes for anything out of place that could alarm us of an enemy presence in the area. My fear subsided as the lead elements of the platoon moved into the jungle, securing our position with a perimeter; it was then I began to feel my exhaustion under the burning sun. Immediately after the perimeter was complete, Lt. Dimagard gave us the order to break for lunch. With everyone's nerves on edge after the vulnerable approach to the trees, most of us went for a cigarette first, before eating any food. Knowing the first several yards inside of a jungle was where the Viet Cong liked to place their booby traps, I cautiously searched for a place to eat my C-Ration and make coffee, painfully careful, looking for trip wires.

The heat dripped sweat from the ends of our noses. I sat on the jungle floor eating lunch with Tom Ziehm, Roy Moseman, Billy Kennington and Moose Johnson, talking about anything but Vietnam. Kennington was a very likable guy from North Carolina, seemingly intelligent and educated, with no brashness about him. He was your average good-looking guy of medium stature; his hair was light blond, his skin reddish tanned. He was intense, but not annoying and his southern roots made him very fond of rolling farmland, hunting and fishing. We were all close friends, but then there was the circle within a circle—a friend you could share anything with, and if the bond was broken by death or being wounded, it was highly unlikely another bond so close could ever be formed again. I saw it in many of the hardened veterans around me who undoubtedly lost their closest friends in combat; they shared little about themselves, communicating only enough to function properly within the platoon.

Kennington and Moseman were both from the south and had become inseparable friends. Kennington always talked about his wife and was real fond of his son. I will never forget, Moseman said to me once, there was a country song out at the time called "Skinny Legs and All"—and in that song there were lyrics "take the one with the skinny legs." Kennington said that every time he and his son were together, driving an old pick-up truck and saw some girls walking down the road, his boy would say, "Daddy, take the one with the skinny legs." Most of the time when Tom and I talked about deer hunting, Moseman and Kennington found their way over to us to share their stories of the hunt, taking us all back home for a brief moment.

I look back now and remember how difficult it was, knowing my wife was so far away, wondering if I would ever see her again. Now, after having children, I can't even imagine the inner turmoil that a combat soldier who has children endures. Not only does he long for the embrace of the woman he loves, but also the scent and sight of his babies, the flesh of his flesh. It must have been overwhelming at times for men such as Kennington, his memories so clear he could almost reach out and touch his son's face. I remember seeing Kennington with tears in his eyes after reading a letter from home. He didn't say much, just handed me the new photograph of his son sent by his wife and with a swipe of the hand, his tears were gone.

Inside I think we were all crying, even when the tears were all dried up. It was a constant, unseen weeping in our souls longing to be home, for which there was no cure, except to survive 365 days in a combat zone. For Billy Don Kennington and the other soldiers with children, under a hail of gun fire, nothing could have been more inspiring to survive than the bright, young and innocent faces of their children waiting for them to come home, to have one more Christmas morning by the tree or one more drive down a dirt country road in the mountains of North Carolina, with "Skinny Legs" playing on the radio.

At the edge of the jungle we looked over a small village, about six hooches, standing in the middle of a clear cut, looking as ancient as 1000 years before. A dirt path ran inside the edge of the jungle, leading to the village a few hundred yards in front of us. I didn't know much about the area, other than overhearing Lt. Dimagard and Sgt. Williams saying the Route 66 canal turned and traveled in close proximity of the village.

The sun was beginning to set when Lt. Dimagard decided to move our platoon into the village. The shadows began to show themselves as we entered. As always, the children flocked around us like sea gulls at the beach, begging for food. Most of the men started handing out candy, but I was quickly escorted to the sick children, freely and ungrudgingly administering immunization shots and aspirin while checking vitals and for symptoms of dehydration. Helping the children always gave me a small amount of quietness in my soul, and in Vietnam, any peace for the soul was welcome, regardless of how short-lived the feeling was. I knew that for every child I helped, there were others dying from sickness and being caught up in bombing runs and firefights. I helped who I could and the village treated me like a God because of the medicine I gave them.

The adults in the village went about their business working in the rice field, drying fishing nets and collecting fruits and vegetables. They didn't really know what to expect when American soldiers entered their village; however, they did

155

know they had to keep all doors open, thus proving their loyalty to our cause, which was helping the ARVN Army and ensuring South Vietnam stayed a democracy. Upon our entrance into their village, they must have felt fear, since all too often our presence instigated deadly firefights directly in and around the villages we searched and visited.

The village chief offered his hooch to Lt. Dimagard to use as our Command Post. It was a large structure, as far as hooches go, made of bamboo and straw, with several brightly colored oriental mats placed neatly on the dry mud floor. I was beside Dimagard, with Overcast, Williams, Moseman and Tom sitting in a semi-circle facing the village chief. The chief's skin was dark, his eyes even darker, but his face had a friendly smile. He sat on one of the mats beside his straw, cone-shaped farming hat, a long pipe smoldered from his lips.

When Ting walked into the hooch, he began conversing with the chief in a calm voice and relayed the information back to Dimagard and Williams. Tom and I were eating with the others and overheard that supposedly there were no Viet Cong in the area. Ting seemed to be convinced, but Dimagard still decided to send out an all night listening post, choosing Tom's 1st squad to go outside the perimeter and of course, I went along as the medic.

After eating inside the Command Post, we had a short briefing with Lt. Dimagard and Sgt. Williams about the night ambush. When we left the hooch, the sun was beginning to settle behind the horizon. The 1st squad fell in behind Tom at the point, rustling through their gear, checking for ammunition, hand grenades and the all important superstitious items which at times seemed as vital to our survival as the weapons we carried. For me, my invisible shield was my small white Bible in the front of my helmet. Others carried crucifixes, photographs, letters and a few men that I knew wore their children's birth bracelets on their wrists.

Tom was ready to move out and while looking back at the men in his squad he said with a clear voice, "Saddle up...Lock and load." Immediately following his order, the quietness of the evening was briefly interrupted from the bolts of our rifles clanging forward with an eerie metal against metal echo, locking and loading the bullets into the chambers of the barrels. The silence returned and Tom turned around, leading us into the black curtain of jungle.

On the point of our squad of about ten men, Tom moved slowly through the dim fading light, cautious of booby traps or any sign of the enemy. The traps could be grenades in the trees with trip wires, bouncing betties, booby trapped claymores or anything else the Viet Cong could get their hands on. Tom searched for a place to set up the ambush. In front of me, Bruce Johnson and Kennington were walking slowly with M-16's swiveling side to side in unison with their heads and eyes. Parham was also there, a red-headed freckled faced black guy from New York, who stuttered when he talked. We all wore flack vests, but because it was so hot and humid, few of us buttoned up the front of the vest.

After only a few minutes into our slow methodical walk, I saw a bright flash and heard a deafening explosion in front of me. I brought my rifle to my shoulder and my heart instantly began to pound as I moved forward. My eyes were nearly blind after the flash of light. I heard cursing and swearing, but couldn't see who it was or who had been hit. When I reached the blast area, my eyes had begun to adjust to the low light and I was met by Parham carrying Moose over his shoulder with both of his legs torn up real bad.

I immediately saw Kennington wounded, lying on the ground, with Tom kneeling beside him. I knelt beside Kennington; he was listless and his eyes were wide. I opened his vest and found no serious wounds, but something was wrong. It looked like he was staring up at the clouds, flat on his back. His vital signs told me I was losing him and I began giving him mouth to mouth and pounded on his chest, but nothing was bringing him around. I quickly focused on his head and noticed two small shrapnel holes at his temple. His eyes were still open, looking far through my eyes, as if I wasn't even there. Then strangely his eyes closed slowly as if he fell to sleep. He became limp in my arms and his life slid away, like steam rising to the sky.

I moved quickly in the black of night to the Command Post to treat Moose Johnson and my heart nearly jumped into my throat, suddenly finding myself frozen, looking down the barrel of a gun held by a GI by the name of Mills. He said, "Fuck Doc, I almost shot ya." Without saying a word I knocked his gun to the side and went to the CP.

Back at the Command Post Moose Johnson was in a lot of pain with shrapnel wounds in both of his lower legs. I quickly gave him morphine, quieting his moans of anguish. Roy Moseman was beside me with a few others giving comfort. For a moment everything had turned to chaos with several other men walking back to the village with shrapnel wounds. Lt. Dimagard was on the radio calling in a boat for medical evacuation. Ting returned from the jungle furious, telling Sgt. Williams it was a handheld device that detonated the booby trap, which meant the enemy was close, operating in or around the village. I had never seen Ting so furious and he quickly took a squad of men and began searching the immediate area for Vietnamese stragglers or possible Viet Cong guerillas.

I could hear the rumble of the Tango boats as they approached nearby for the evacuation and quickly gave Moose a slap on the shoulder and told him, "I wish I was going with you, ya lucky son of a bitch," and said good-bye to him. I immediately went with a small squad of men back to Kennington's body which had begun to cool. I collected his personal items: a final letter to his family, his wallet, and a photograph of his beloved son. I placed them in my bag to turn in to the Senior Medic of Charlie Company. A deep sickness came over me as I tagged his body and covered him with a poncho liner. Tom and Moseman helped me carry the body to the canal where I placed him in a body bag and we loaded him into the Tango boat for the voyage back to America.

The Mobile Riverine Force took us back to Dong Tam. This time it was without Kennington. In my mind I can still see the look of melancholy on his face after reading letters from his wife and son. I can still see Kennington eating C-Rations leaning up against a tree next to Tom, Moose and his closest friend Roy Moseman. I can still see his eyes slowly close as he died in my arms. It was just another day in the Nam. But for us, the men of the 2nd Platoon, it was a day of great loss.

For me—Billy Don Kennington was the first close friend I had lost. I had seen many men killed, but this was different—we ate, drank, slept and fought together. Coming in from that mission, I recall a gut wrenching emptiness in my soul, knowing a mother and a child would soon receive the news of his death. I was filled with a flood of questions about the purpose and cost of the war, and without digging very deep inside my soul, I knew this would not be the last friend I would lose. My eyes were beginning to open to the depth of the friendships around me—the once strangers that I fought beside. The political motivations and questions in my mind fled like dust in the wind.

I realized what I was fighting for—we were all fighting for each other. I was not only fighting to save my own life, but my brothers around me and in return, they did the same for me. Deep inside I knew if I were lying in the middle of a field bleeding to death, under a hail of bullets—I would not want anyone to commit suicide in a vain attempt to save my life. But that is just what made our brotherhood so close, because even deeper in my soul, I knew they would enter the field to save my life anyways. In that depth between men, I saw a piece of the wheel fade away to death in the eye's of Billy Don Kennington. By the greatest of all standards and definition, we lost a brother that day. The death of Kennington brought all of our rage to a breaking point.

Roy Moseman told me at a reunion decades after the war, he became depressed for several days. After the death of Kennington, he returned home and looked at his friends in a different way. He was made aware of the shallowness of his new friendships compared to those in Vietnam.

Roy Moseman said years after the war:

"They had not gotten far from us when we heard the explosion. Then we heard the bad news over the field radio. Billy Kennington had been killed and Bruce Johnson had been badly wounded. I don't know how they got Kennington out, but I remember Parham carrying Johnson back over his shoulders. We had a Tango boat pick him up on the river-bank and take him to the hospital ship. I never saw Johnson again, until about 10 years ago, when we had our 1995 Mobile Riverine Force Association reunion in Louisville, Kentucky. He was wounded in both knees, but recovered pretty well. It still makes me sad to this day when I think about him. I think of his son and that song, "Skinny Legs and All." Kennington was the first one of our men I saw killed and it really hurt me. Two of our guys, Teddy Toth and Ed Lapuski said that they had seen enough. They refused to go on any more missions and both were sent to Long Bhen Jail. They did about two months in jail and came back to the unit. As far as I know they made it home alive."

We were all brothers in the most literal way—a way understood only by the combat veteran. The greatest standard can be found in the Bible in John 15:13—"Greater love has no one, than this, that he lay down his life for his friends." That is exactly how we looked at Kennington—whether directly or indirectly it may have been—he did not die for some political achievement; he died for us—his brothers. He took the shrapnel for us. In a million

times a million lifetimes, I will never forget Billy
Don Kennington.

Billy Don Kennington

The Cross Roads

Soon after the death of Billy Don Kennington, I was appointed to Senior Medic of Charlie Company. I was then responsible for keeping all the other medics in the company supplied with medical tools, bandages, ointments, Darvocet and morphine. When new medics arrived, I gave them a quick introduction to the Nam.

I remember a new medic from the 1st Platoon coming to see me; his skin was pale white, with big scared eyes, just in from the world. Like all new guys, he was looking for a friend and asking a lot of questions. I told him what I could, but ultimately combat was the greatest teacher. If a medic froze during combat, he wasn't around very long. I recall looking at him in his unstained jungle clothes, almost feeling sorry for him. There were many new guys coming into Charlie Company, but that one medic stayed with me all these years.

Once again, the barracks ship towered over me under a dim red spot light, as a cloud of diesel fumes drifted across my face. I walked down the steep steel stairs of our USS Colleton, preparing to load into one of the several Tango boats, filled with the same gut wrenching anxiety that all missions inflicted upon me. What seemed like chaos around me was actually a very organized mustering of hundreds of infantry soldiers, organized by platoons, loading into the boats.

Before long, our convoy pulled away from the barge planks and entered the eerie, graveyard currents of the Song My Tho River. It was a large operation, including both Bravo and Charlie Companies. The Mekong River was several hundred yards wide outside Dong Tam and the brown color of the water was hidden under the darkness of a sunless sky. The massive silhouette of the USS Colleton faded away behind us.

I was filled with apprehension. There was no laughing or joking. I sat across from Tom, recalling scripture from my white Bible. My most comforting verse was Psalm 23: "Yea, though I walk through the valley of the shadow of death, I will fear no evil: for thou art with me; thy rod and thy staff they comfort me." I knew the Bible well. Even though I had the small book open before me under darkness, I wasn't actually reading it. I had long before memorized the verses.

Sgt. Williams talked candidly with us in an effort to ease our raddled nerves. Lt. Dimagard was on the radio with Overcast beside him holding the radio unit on his back. Death was always in the air over Vietnam, but that morning it shrouded our two infantry battalions ready to strike. I remember the strangeness in the air, almost a sixth sense that we just knew not everyone was coming back alive. How and where the enemy would hit us, we didn't know, but the feeling of dread was among us that morning and it was thick. The Cross Roads was a "Hell of Place."

Tom always sat across from me, his tall lanky body half slouched in the bench seat. We looked at each other through the darkness, with no words, only stone faces, filled with fear and question staring back at each other for nearly an hour. Then, the violet light of dawn began to peak over the black wall of jungle along the river's edge and the faces around me became more clear.

Bravo Company was in front, the last of their boats was a heavily armed Alpha boat. We turned into a canal only seventy yards wide and at times even narrower. I looked out and saw nothing but dense jungle. The two Navy gunners stood behind their 50 calibers, waiting and praying. The landing was to take place only a short distance before the Cross Roads itself, where the jungle was thick and unforgiving on both sides. I couldn't see ten feet into the jungle and we all felt we were being watched, striking us with familiar dread.

It was mid-morning when we approached the Landing Zone and nobody muttered a single word. Lt. Dimagard stood poised and Sgt. Williams slowly moved through the troop bay, slapping men on the shoulder and on the helmet. The canvas canopy over our heads hid us from the morning sunlight, but heat and humidity was already pressing upon us. The stone faces around me looked empty, but in reality we were far from empty, rather filled with a thousand thoughts and emotions.

Bravo's Tango boats began to move into position and I heard the diesel engines change momentum. The boats turned hard right, pointing their bows toward the shoreline. The monitor boats halted and waited with guns facing the shorelines, ready to unleash their enormous firepower. Our boat was heading toward the shore when all hell broke loose. Enemy machine gun fire opened up on Bravo Company. Instantly, all the big guns in the convoy were screaming. The 20-millimeter cannons on my boat shook the troop bay like an earth quake. I could see nothing from inside, but the sound of war was all around me, continuous ear splitting gunfire and incoming rocket fire spit through the air. I listened to the carnage, knowing the gate would soon lower onto the shore, leaving us in the middle of it all.

The radio unit on Overcast's back squelched out with the screams of dying and wounded and fighting men. All I could think about was "Get me off this fucking boat." The gate began to drop before us and I took in one last breath, thinking it might be my last. Sgt. Williams yelled out over the sounds of war, with anger in his face, "Let's un-ass this mother fucker."

Armored Troop Carrier or Tango boat as the
GI's called them. Notice the landing ramp and
troop bay with canopy in the front.

I was in the middle of the platoon, stricken with
adrenaline, watching the men unload before me,
clanging with equipment, low to the ground,
running for cover. The instinct for survival became
greater than our fears. The darkness under the boat
canopy was gone as I ran off the edge of the landing
ramp. With tunnel vision I followed Tom to the
jungle's edge, throwing myself to the ground behind
the first tree I came to. Small arms fire opened up
on our position, splitting the air over my head with

a whistle. We were only a few yards from the canal, our faces buried into the jungle floor.

Seconds after taking cover, with no specific enemy target, I lifted my gun and started shooting back at the sound of enemy fire. Lt. Dimagard and Overcast were a few yards away next to a small clump of trees trying to call in fire support, but he soon realized the enemy was too close. For the artillery to be effective, it would have had to be dropped nearly on top of us.

Fighting for their lives in close combat, Bravo Company was taking the brunt of the ambush across the canal behind me. But for those that were still alive, as their saving grace, two helicopter gunships entered the theatre of war, flying low over the water. The choppers nosed down almost to a complete stop, simultaneously unleashing rockets over Bravo Company's heads—silencing the enemy machine gun position. Immediately, with the arrival of the helicopters, the hail of enemy gunfire lifted from us and into the air at the choppers. The gunfire directed toward the choppers was snuffed out by the Monitor and Alpha boats; their 40mm and 20mm cannons and their massive 81mm mortars began firing for effect. The enemy positions that were about 75 yards in front of me were turned into a rubbish pile of explosions and burning jungle.

Only the canal separated our companies as we fought back to back, with each second becoming more lethal for the Viet Cong. The enemy had no choice but to focus on the helicopters, allowing us—two entire infantry companies - to concentrate our firepower. Over two hundred American soldiers lashed out with M-60 machine guns, M-16s and grenade launchers. Behind us, the riverine boats continued ripping down the jungle and the enemy inside of it. The Viet Cong were forced to flee and the chaos ended. Although the Viet Cong pulled back deeper into the jungle, sporadic sniper fire still echoed out in the distance.

With both Landing Zones secure, a deafening silence fell upon us. My adrenaline began to lower with the help of a cigarette and I began to realize how fortunate my platoon was, sustaining only a couple minor shrapnel wounds. Charlie Company as a whole was lucky, with none of our 3 platoons having anyone killed in action, but for Bravo Company it was a much different story.

Sgt. Williams walked up to Tom and I as we sat on the ground, our backs against a couple of trees, chain smoking another cigarette. He told me Bravo Company needed every available medic across the canal. All I wanted to do was keep smoking and make some coffee, but I knew they were hit hard after hearing the ambush over the radio.

I took a Tango boat to the other side of the canal, knowing the focus of the ambush fell on Bravo Company. Several black plumes of smoke ascended into the air and I could smell the death ahead of me. I stepped off the boat and was greeted by a soldier covered in blood; his face was absent minded, showing only pure exhaustion. I empathized with him without saying any words, knowing underneath his fatigue was frustration and rage. I slapped him lightly on the shoulder, looking him in the eyes, assuring him I knew what he was feeling. As he turned away, gesturing for me to follow, I noticed the back of his neck was smeared with blood, most likely from swatting at mosquitoes while trying to save the wounded. I stayed close behind him while walking through a narrow strip of flattened grass along the canal. To the left of us was nothing but dense jungle.

Soon, one of the black plumes of smoke was upon us, which turned out to be an enemy machine gun nest just off the bow of a Tango boat. I looked inside the hull of the boat, having dropped its landing ramp only 10 yards in front of the barrels of the enemy machine gun, the platoon of men were ambushed at point blank range. They never had a chance. The hull was draining several inches of blood and water and at the end of the landing ramp, nearly a dozen filled body bags laid neatly in a row. The wounded had already been pulled out. I looked around me and every standing tree in the area had a wounded man leaning against it. I began talking to the wounded, checking their vitals, administering pain medicine and replacing blood saturated bandages.

The casualties that Bravo Company sustained were not solely at the Landing Zone, men were killed and wounded inside the jungle as well, leaving blood trails heading in many different directions. Near the water, where the helicopters unleashed their rockets, the Viet Cong machine gun position was reduced to torn trees, burned foliage and ashes smoldering with the smell of burning flesh and the "rotten egg stench" of explosives. At the core of it all were several enemy soldiers scorched to little more than skeletal remains.

Bravo Company secured a Landing Zone for evacuation in a rice paddy nearby. I didn't know the dead and wounded personally and I don't remember their names, but there were many, perhaps a dozen or more killed and the wounded were everywhere—some were walking and others barely clinging to life. There were different wounds: sucking chest, legs and arms held on by only ligaments. I worked on the wounded with blood stained hands. My mind blocked out the horror of it all. I was just going through the motions, applying pressure dressings, tourniquets, checking vitals and giving morphine.

I stood next to Bravo Company's Senior Medic as he reported the nature of the wounds to the incoming Dustoff chopper—allowing the medics aboard to prepare. As we loaded the first chopper with the wounded, a sniper began shooting in our direction, but it wasn't very close and without incident the helicopter lifted into the air. The other medics and I felt the thankfulness of the wounded—even from those that were unable to speak. I looked at a man lying in the chopper, torn up, unable to speak. The chopper was only a second away from lifting and the man tried to raise his hand to give a gesture of thanks, but I gently pushed his hand down, giving him rest. His eyes were calm looking into mine and he knew I heard his unspoken words.

After the last helicopters flew in and the dead were loaded, I rinsed the blood from my hands. I took a Tango boat back across the canal, returning to Charlie Company. I found Lt. Dimagard and the others from my platoon strung out in linear fashion along a path, sitting down, eating an early lunch. We had secured the area, but sniper fire was pestering us, keeping us low to the ground and eating our lunch lying down, preferably behind a tree.

Mid-afternoon we were still taking sporadic sniper fire. 1st Platoon was on point in front of us. We moved not far from the canal, easing our way along a narrow dirt path, cutting under an ancient canopy of jungle. Usually during the afternoon Lt. Dimagard gave us a break, letting us heat up coffee and smoke a cigarette, but that day we stayed silent, moving as little as possible, eating only a chocolate bar and a few slow sips from the canteen.

By late afternoon the path we traveled intersected another dirt path, bringing us to the edge of a rubber tree plantation. I was in the middle of the platoon, creeping along the path with my head on a swivel, listening to the other platoons chattering over the radio. The 1st Platoon began taking on sniper fire just as we entered a clearing with a small hooch resting inside of it. One side of the path led toward the canal and the other turned slightly around the clearing and the hooch, leading into the plantation. We knelt in silence, waiting for the 1st Platoon to move out again, but the snipers were still firing, keeping them pinned down.

We had been pestered all day with sniper fire, but luckily our company hadn't taken any serious casualties. The Viet Cong would only snipe for a few minutes before falling further back into the jungle, preventing us from pinpointing their location and calling in a dozen bombs on top of them. When the shooting stopped it became silent, the only thing heard was the whisper of radio chatter and Lt. Dimagard softly answering back. On a few occasions at a far distance near the Landing Zones across the canal, we heard Bravo Company's guns scream out in small firefights, followed by mortar explosions delivered by the riverine boats. One thing was for sure—the enemy was all over the place and we had no idea how many were out there.

A few hundred meters in front of us, the 1st Platoon reported over the radio they were on their feet, moving slowly, somewhere inside the rubber tree plantation. The jungle around us became eerily silent without even the slightest chirp of a bird. Lt.

Dimagard and Sgt. Williams were conversing on how to handle the intersecting paths and after a brief discussion they decided to clear the inside of the hooch by sending a squad to our right flank. The open terrain was vulnerable to cross, as were all clearings that rested near the edge of dense tree cover. Nobody liked crossing fields or clear cuts. On top of that, we had been making contact with the enemy all day, which only made the apprehension worse.

A muted bitching and cursing softly echoed through the ranks of the platoon when Sgt. Williams chose the squad to move out on our right flank. I couldn't blame them—I sure as hell didn't want to go near the hooch either. The squad of about ten men quietly broke off from our platoon and flanked down the path toward the hooch. Parham was one of the lead men in the squad. I watched him move at a moderate pace off the path, heading directly at the hooch. Suspiciously, Parham walked into the hooch. Instantly, automatic gunfire opened up, breaking the silence. Parham ran out of the hooch in a state of panic, stumbling, falling and yelling, "They're in the fucking hooch." Without hesitation, Wilbanks opened up on the hooch with the machine gun, along with most of the others in the platoon firing their M-16's. As the firefight raged on, Parham continued to run in a fanatic frenzy, bleeding heavily from both of his legs.

With the help of Roy Moseman, I tackled him to the jungle floor and tried to calm him down. While I began working on Parham's wounds, one of the Viet Cong made a run for the trees but was cut down immediately, falling into a bloody heap on the jungle floor. With lightning speed, the second enemy soldier ran out of the hooch and everyone started shooting again, striking him somewhere in the upper torso near the shoulder, spinning and tumbling him to the ground. But he stood again and continued running, disappearing into the jungle and the fading light of dusk.

Parham was shot in both of his lower legs several times. Panic stricken and in pain, with Moseman holding him down, I continued to work on him. Cutting off his pant legs, I realized he was torn up pretty good with one of the bullets hitting the bone. After settling him down with a shot of morphine, I looked down at him with a semi-grin, "You're about to get the fuck out of here," and with a morphine high, he smiled back.

Several GI's approached the dead body cautiously and also found a blood trail from the second enemy soldier that escaped, but nobody was about to go chasing after a wounded Viet Cong through the jungle. One of the men in the squad moved up beside the body with his gun ready to fire and placed his foot underneath it, rolling the body over face up. He yelled out, "Mother Fucker Parham...yur ass got shot by a woman." While wrapping both of Parham's tattered lower legs, he said, "Cock suck'n bitch, I can't believe I got hit by a woman, a fuck'n woman." His words were fierce, but the half grin on his freckled face told me he was happier than a pig in shit, knowing he was going home!

Darkness was coming over us quickly and the wounded had to be evacuated. The 1st Platoon had a couple of men critically wounded and we were a long way from any fields to bring in the choppers. Not only was it dangerous for us to seek out a clearing in the dark with an unknown amount of Viet Cong in the area, but also, if some of the wounded weren't in surgery within the hour, they would surely die. We had to make a quick decision and burning down the hooch near the rubber plantation would give us just enough area to bring in a helicopter.

After securing the perimeter, we pulled out Zippo lighters and lit the straw hooch in all four corners. Within minutes the flames were blazing with sparks ascending high above the trees, revealing our exact position to the enemy. We knew the Viet Cong would figure out we were making a Landing Zone and would go to great lengths to take down a helicopter. As the structure burned, we cut down a few small trees that remained in the clearing and expanded our perimeter to try and prevent the enemy from getting within lethal range of the Landing Zone. Within minutes the burning straw hooch was reduced to smolder and over the radio I relayed the nature of the wounds to the medics inside the chopper, preparing them as much as possible.

The helicopter was upon us, hovering over the tree line. With the wounded beside me, I held a red strobe light in the black of night, directing the pilot into the clearing. As the helicopter lowered to the ground, kicking up ash and debris, the coals under our feet and beneath the wounded men turned cherry hot and flames began shooting up inside the Landing Zone, ignited from the rush of air created by the helicopter blades. Some of the wounded were panicked like everyone else and some were unconscious from the loss of blood, clueless to the threat of burning to death. We were forced to send the chopper out of the Landing Zone and we carried the dead and wounded off the flaming hot coals.

Once again, where the hooch had stood was glowing with flames against a wall of darkness. We rushed over and began scooping water out of two clay pots that stood beside the hooch before we burned it. Adding to the chaos, the pilots radioed to us they were taking on heavy sniper fire from our north. Every second was critical to the wounded men and the lives of the pilots, hovering like sitting ducks in a pond. The most prevalent thought in my mind was "I got to get these guys the fuck out of here." A steady line of helmets filled with water quickly put the flames out allowing us to bring the chopper in a second time. The chopper hovered higher in the air this time and just as the coals began to turn hot again the pilot stopped his descent, forcing us to pick the dead and wounded up over our shoulders to slide them into the chopper.

A great relief came over me as the chopper pulled out and headed back to Dong Tam. But my relief was short lived as we listened to enemy gun fire a few hundred yards away shooting at the helicopter. The jungle became silent once again and the radio checks were the only sounds I heard. GI's slowly moved to their place on the perimeter for the night whispering "You fuck'n believe that shit?"

Our Command Post for the night was set and each squad placed trip flares and claymores across their positions out on the perimeter. I sat quietly talking to Lt. Dimagard, Sgt. Williams and Overcast inside the CP. I could finally breathe for a moment after a day of constant harassment by the enemy. The exhaustion made even my steel helmet feel like a pillow from home, but the jungle and its moving shadows was my true reality. Somewhere out there was an unknown amount of Viet Cong—and they were close, having watched us all day, shooting at us whenever possible. I had a strange feeling, as if the enemy was sucking us deeper into the jungle, beyond escape.

Night had come over us. I watched Dimagard and Williams scouring a map with a red lens flashlight, a poncho half pulled over their bodies to hide even the dullest of light. Overcast worked the radio, checking in with the squads on the perimeter saying,

"2-1...2-6... is everything clear?" After a brief moment the squad returned a single squelch indicating everything was cool. The radio checks continued every half hour and all of us inside the CP took turns working the radio in 2 hour shifts, affording us some sleep through the night.

I was lying on my back, my head resting on my helmet, when one of our squads reported movement on the perimeter. Within seconds our entire platoon was alerted and ready—about forty men loaded to the hilt with M-16's, M-60 machine guns and grenade launchers. With great anxiety we waited for one of the trip flares to illuminate on the perimeter, but there was nothing. After fifteen minutes of staring into darkness, Tom Ziehm reported they no longer saw any movement in front of them.

Without warning, about seventy yards beside us, 1st Platoon's trip flares illuminated, followed immediately by a hail of automatic gun fire with green and red tracer bullets exchanging back and forth—the green indicating our gunfire and the red tracers the Viet Cong's. Our 1st and 2nd squads opened up with a quick burst of automatic fire toward the flashes of red tracers and then silenced their guns for a radio check. Seconds after our burst of fire, the 1st Platoon reported our line of fire was clear, eliminating any worries about us shooting

180

anyone from our own company. With the green light for go, Wilbanks raged on the M-60 and all guns were blazing, barrels hot, along with Sanky Thomas dropping M-79 grenades into the enemy position. The enemy answered us with a small volume of return fire, but our 1st and 2nd squads changed their positions slightly and punched back, silencing the enemy's fire toward our platoon.

The burst of fire by the enemy tapered down as our entire company fired back. We filled the hours of darkness with brilliant crossing streaks of red and green tracers. The gunfire often slowed down to sporadic pocket fire from the 1st Platoon, but it wasn't long before the earth and air shook again with the sound of war. The Viet Cong were everywhere and by the angle of some of the red tracers being fired toward us, we could tell some of the Viet Cong were even hiding in the tree tops. After a sustained length of pure chaos, both sides shooting, bullets thudding the ground and zipping over our heads, the sounds of war lowered again, returning to small firefights along the 1st Platoon's far side perimeter over a hundred yards away.

We continued listening to small firefights along 1st Platoon's perimeter, unable to see very much except for the occasional streaks of green and red tracers too far away to help return fire. Then, when the fighting seemed to be almost over, our trip flares went off near Tom's 1st squad and the night lit up again with maddening chaos. Directly into our position enemy fire pounded us, bullets splitting the air over our heads and shredding the foliage growing from the jungle floor.

We were forced to pull back a short distance into the ditches of a banana grove, to give us more cover from the steady volume of enemy fire. The 1st and 2nd squads were now only a stone's throw away from the CP. Tom Ziehm came over to us fairly calm, telling us "They're all over the fucking place." Roscoe had followed Tom into the Command Post in a panicked frenzy, repeatedly yelling, "Charlie's got his shit together this time…it's all over now." Roscoe was so unhinged Tom grabbed him by the face and told him, "Shut the fuck up Roscoe." Ting, Sgt. Williams, Lt Dimagard, Overcast, Moseman and Sgt. Maynard were all trying to figure out what our next move should be. The deafening blast of fire aimed at us stopped as quickly as it began, but the Viet Cong didn't stop shooting, rather they redirected their fire back into the 1st Platoon and all we could do was listen to the horror unfold. I knew the 1st Platoon was getting hurt badly and we were helpless, unable to call in air support because the enemy was almost on top of us.

Years after the war, Roy Moseman said, "Charlie was all around us, in the bushes and even in the trees. He had us pinned down and right where he wanted us." And he was exactly right—all day long the Viet Cong were harassing us, figuring out our movements, waiting for darkness to attack and get close enough to make artillery and fire-support useless.

We heard the final hours of the battle and listened to the men screaming over the radio. Unable to bring helicopters into the area, we knew the critically wounded wouldn't make it through the night. Sometime in the early predawn hours the enemy left, leaving behind an eerie silence.

At dawn, a heavy fog hung in the air. The morning smelled of sweat, death and gunpowder. The palm trees and foliage were tattered and torn by bullets and shrapnel. Brass bullet casings littered the ground around me. When we moved into the 1st Platoon's position, the ground was not only littered with brass bullet casings but also the dead and wounded. Some of the wounded rested against trees, letting out blood with their tourniquets every few minutes. It was then when I noticed the new medic I had equipped with medical gear just days before the operation curled in a fetal position. He was so young, so pale and so dead. Beside him was a sergeant stretched out on the ground, in his hand was an undetonated claymore mine device. They were all dead. Everywhere I looked was a dead body. At first glance they appeared to be sleeping peacefully, but a closer look showed the bloating of their bodies and the insects feeding on them.

I took dog tags and covered them with poncho liners, noticing several of the dead could have been saved if helicopter evacuation would have been possible. I was covered in blood, but it was like mechanic's grease. The mind has a way of blocking things out. I remember sitting in the Tango boat on our way back to Dong Tam; it was quiet and I was exhausted emotionally and physically. I kept thinking, "Oh my God, I made it."

We stood on the barge beside the barracks ship waiting in line to get the mud hosed off our legs and feet. When the hose hit my clothing a slight crimson blood seeped its way out. One thing the Navy liked was a clean ship. On the ship each of us were given two beers. I recall drinking them quietly, thinking about the dead. Regardless of my thoughts, I was unable to feel any emotion. It was like I was an empty shell, my insides hollow. I knew the fear of combat would return, but sadness seemed to be fleeting. The dead seemed to be at peace and the survivors continued in torment.

Assholes and Elbows

It was the second day of a mission somewhere in the Mekong. We were covered in mud and rancid water, our faces were semi distorted with bumps from mosquito bites. The boats dropped us off at the Cross Roads again. It felt like we were returning to the seen of a crime. All the platoons of Charlie Company moved in close proximity to each other. My platoon was in the center of the sweeping operation and I could see the 1st Platoon to my left every so often. We crossed a rice field, holding tight to a tree line along a ditch that provided somewhat dry ground to walk on. It was late morning when our quiet walk ended with several snipers opening up on us.

Our entire Company was pinned down and took cover in the drainage ditch that ran the edge of the rice field. Tom and I were next to each other, our heads and arms exposed at the top of the mounded bank of the ditch. With water up to our waists it was an agonizing stalemate with sucking leeches and mosquitoes, while bullets sporadically raked the mud in front of us. The sniper picked his way around aiming at targets of opportunity, but most of the platoon was submerged in water, utilizing the full coverage of the mounded ditch.

While the sniper focused on the forward elements of our platoon, Tom and I crawled out of the water and rested on top of the furrow, trying to stay as dry as possible. The sniper's bullets thudded and sprayed mud in the air several yards away near

Roy Moseman. There was a brief silence, with only the sound of sloshing mud and cursing inside the trench. The silence was soon interrupted from a distance as the sniper focused on the 1st Platoon. I stared into Tom's eyes with a look of, "Get me the fuck out of here."

Comfortably, Tom and I rested on the ditch mound for another fifteen minutes, still with our head and shoulders exposed, preventing our legs and feet from being submerged with the leeches. Suddenly the mud began to thump and spatter near us, hitting several feet away from our heads. Within seconds, the sniper fire quickly closed in on us as the enemy found us as his mark. Bullets pelted the earth inches away from our heads, splattering mud in our faces. I was frozen with fear, unable to move, thinking if I moved, I would move right into the enemy's bullets. "Holy shit he's shooting at me," I thought. At the same time, while looking at each other in the face, Tom and I slid further into the ditch, saturating the rest of our bodies with muddy water.

After being pinned down for several hours, I heard a Cayuse helicopter inbound and watched it land behind the tree-line at the rear of our platoon, far from the threat of the sniper. Stepping off the chopper was a man in crisp, clean fatigues and dark sunglasses, carrying a black gun case. Greeted by Sgt. Williams, the American sniper opened the case and pulled out an M-14 rifle with an enormous scope on top. He followed Williams into the ditch and they began sloshing toward me with their heads below the crest of the mound. They moved past me a few yards to Lt. Dimagard, where Sgt. Williams showed him the general direction of the enemy sniper.

The American sniper pulled out a spotting scope and began searching the distant jungle. After several minutes he finally spoke, saying, "I got your sniper....he's smoking a cigarette right now." He pulled his M-14 up to his shoulder with a calmness that demanded the attention of everyone. He adjusted his scope and then settled his shoulder into the stock of his weapon. His rifle CRACKED out with a single shot. He paused for a second, still looking through his scope, and then relaxed his M-14 rifle back inside the confines of the ditch. "He won't be bothering ya no more," he said calmly with a grin. He coolly put his equipment back in the case, walked back to the chopper and was gone.

The freedom of movement was embraced, but it only meant we would be moving deeper into the jungle. After the sniper was killed, I was called over to the 1st Platoon, where a lieutenant had been wounded. Normally their medic would be called up, but since I was closer it was more practical to send me. The rest of my platoon was saddling up to move out when I came upon a man wounded in the abdomen by the name Lt. Page. As I pulled up his shirt I could hardly believe my eyes; his belt buckle diverted the bullet, leaving nothing more than a nasty scratch. "You're one lucky fucker Lieutenant," I said. I told him to keep the wound covered and clean and slapped him on the shoulder. He thanked me and I quickly returned to my platoon.

The remaining hours of daylight were spent searching for the enemy. It was humid and hard to breathe. Once again, our clothes dried with a stench. We still had several small canals to cross before we set up for the night. Before crossing the first canal, I prepared my gear and slid into the water, covering my back with a thick coat of mud and saturating once again my recently dried clothes. Only the point man got mud on his chest; once he was out of the canal, he turned around and handed the GI behind him his gunstock and pulled him out. It wasn't easy, but we were becoming good at functioning under complete exhaustion.

After about an hour I was getting ready to jump into the last canal as one of the new guys in front of me climbed out of a ditch and handed his gun to the man behind him. He never put his gun on safe and the GI in the canal clipped the trigger. All I heard was a short burst of rounds on full automatic. Several men faintly yelled out for a medic, as if there was no need for me to hurry, but I did anyway and had quickly reached the other side of the canal. I knew immediately why the cry for medic was so half-hearted. I had hoped it was because there were no serious injuries, but instead I found a fresh, new face, with a dozen bullet holes in his chest, killed by his own gun. His eyes were already glassing over. I collected his personal belongings, pulled his dog tags and put a poncho liner over him. He hadn't even been in Vietnam long enough to have a good-bye letter written.

No one thought it was anybody else's fault. The tragedy was just a mistake, made by a young man who hadn't been there long enough—his gun should have been on safe and the barrel he was gripping should have been off to the side. I just shook my head and said "What a fucking waste," and called for a helicopter to come and get him.

When dusk approached the company halted. I was with Tom's squad on the perimeter preparing for the night. Wilbanks was going over his machine gun, aiming it down a narrow walking path that traveled along a canal. It seemed there was a canal everywhere we went on a mission. Shlogal was blowing up his air mattress. Tom was going through his pack, getting ready for dinner. In his pack was a tightly wrapped hammock made of rope that he slept in. I remember we were bartering for meals, peaches and pound cake was our favorite and was a big ticket item for trading C-Rations. We continued talking shit and exchanging insults to pass the time and the sun was nearly behind the trees.

Instantly, like the turning of a light switch, with as much speed as the human body could possibly move, it was assholes and elbows grabbing for our guns. I dropped my meal; Tom threw his pack; Shlogal pushed his air mattress away; and Wilbank lunged for his M-60 machine gun as a squad of three Viet Cong soldiers walked in on us. Seeing each other at the same time, the dusk sky turned into a rage of fire and illuminating tracer rounds.

Our initial burst of fire hit the lead enemy soldier in the chest, blowing him back off his feet. His AK-47 was still firing as he fell to the ground. The other two soldiers disappeared, but we continued to fire until our guns were empty. As Shlogal, Tom and I reloaded, Wilbanks still barked with his M-60 machine gun. We started shooting again for several minutes beside Wilbanks, who was nearly burning the barrel up on his machine gun, until it became obvious the Viet Cong had left or were killed. When Wilbanks finally stopped firing, we could hear Sgt. Williams screaming over the radio. "2-2 What the fuck's going on over there?…What the fuck?…Hold your position, I'm coming the fuck over."

Sgt. Williams was met by all of us, wide eyed and rambling on, "You fuckin believe that shit? Mother fucker… cock suckers." We showed Williams the dead soldier and continued to search for more. We found a heavy blood trail through the jungle and began to follow it. The hunt was overwhelming for all of us. With each and every step along the blood trail the fear was so excruciating it was hard for me to put one foot in front of the other. It was like my legs were freezing up or God was holding us all back and saying, "Not tonight boys, heaven's door is closed." We were certain the man would die, if not dead already, but it was the one that got away unharmed we were worried about. After a few more minutes of searching the immediate area, Sgt. Williams was convinced the third man got away and Lt. Dimagard called us in and said to check it out in the morning.

We went back to camp and slowly the adrenaline began to lower in my body. I placed a poncho liner over the dead Viet Cong soldier and then sat down next to Tom, Shlogal and Wilbanks in a semi-circle facing the direction where the enemy had approached. Sgt. Williams stood over us trying to listen to the four of us rambling on at the same time. Under the darkness we navigated through our gear with red lens flashlights. Shlogal started blowing up his air mattress again and we all heard air escaping through bullet holes. A flush look of 'Oh my God,' came over his face. Tom started unraveling his tightly wrapped hammock and soon realized with each pull of rope, it was in pieces, shredded from bullets. Then as we looked at each other in awe of our survival, I went to open my C-Ration and noticed a bullet had pierced my peaches and pound cake. We looked at each other under the faint glow of red and realized how close death had come to us. It seemed bullets had hit everywhere but where we sat. Sgt. Williams smirked as he witnessed the carnage of the firefight and as he left, he roughly rubbed me on the head saying, "Enough of that shit... I want to go back and eat." On his way back to the CP, he grabbed the dead Viet Cong soldier and pulled him into taller grass so we didn't have to look at him.

We slept that night with one man taking turns at the watch. On my watch the jungle played tricks with my mind—first I thought, "No way in hell is the enemy going to come back at us." Then my mind changed and I thought, "What if he goes back and tells a bunch of his buddies?" My mind went back and forth for my entire watch, along with my eyes distorting tree branches and bushes into human-like figures creeping through the darkness. Finally the morning came, bringing rest to all of my senses.

We loaded back into the Tango boats thankful to be alive. It wasn't long until the rumbling diesel engines brought us back to the Song My Tho River. Resting in the wide brown waters was the secure sight of the Flotilla. The motherships of the Mobile Riverine Force and the roar of Dong Tam was around me. We docked alongside the USS Colleton, and stepped on the barge. Like dogs before they come inside a house, the mud was hosed off us. Once again, we hit the showers and grabbed a hot Navy meal. Our fears were calmed for the time being. Tom walked around in cut-off shorts and sandals, trying to dry out the jungle-rot that was starting to scar his legs. Everyone was either writing a letter to home, playing cards or paying special attention to any pestering wounds and infections. The air conditioning on the ship brought exhaustion quickly and we slept with no thoughts of the next mission—only thoughts of home.

Boats of the Mobile Riverine Force docked beside the USS Colleton.

Eating chow in the jungle: From the front, Tom
Ziehm, Doc MacSwan, Sgt. Williams, Gerald
Elfman and Bruce Johnson.

The Plain of Reeds

Before the lights were out Sgt. Williams brought the orders from Lt. Dimagard saying, "0500 we're moving out," and that was all I knew about the mission ahead of us. Nobody knew anything, except we were moving out—that alone sunk a deep dread into all of us knowing every mission we had recently been on, had engaged the enemy. Before I went to sleep, I wrote a final letter home in case I didn't make it back. I had written one earlier in my tour, but after everything I had been through, I wanted to add to it - not just how much I loved my family back home, but also include the friends I had made in Vietnam and the unique closeness of our friendship and brotherhood. The Book of John says it all, "Greater love has no one than this: to lay down one's life for one's friends."

After three months of combat, I still felt fear before a mission, but also an overwhelming sense of determination—a mission was like a stepping stone to home. Late that night on the boat, I talked quietly to Tom Ziehm, sharing childhood stories. Finally after an hour, we talked ourselves tired and hit our racks. Before sleep came, my thoughts were of home and I conversed with God as if he was visible, sitting beside me. And then I slept.

March 28, 1968:

"Get your asses up… Tangos are ready to load," Sgt. Williams yelled out. There was always a serious look on his face before a mission. His black face looked hard, but his eyes were as if saying, "Mother fucker, lets bring it back in one piece, one more time." It was silent in our birthing area with just the shuffle of everyone grabbing gear. Apprehension quickly fell on me, as if someone was pressing down on my inner being with a hot iron.

I stood on the pontoon barge tied to the barracks ship. It was a large operation, consisting of our entire battalion with an armada of Tango boats idling in the water, smogging the air with diesel fumes. I walked behind Tom and stepped on the floating dock that led to the boat, climbed over the side, and down the short ladder into the troop bay. I took my seat and rested my head back against the boat. Once again I started a small conversation with God.

It was still dark when we pulled away from the mothership. Our destination was a place called the "Plain of Reeds." I never heard anything about the place before and could only wonder how I would remember it. Inside the Tango there was a small hatch and while looking into it I could see the Navy crewmen in the fore of the boat. The diesel engines rumbled the silent morning and the exhaust sent a cloud of moisture lifting from the rear of the boats into the air. Out of the back of the boat, I could see the rest falling in behind us, including a heavily armed Alpha boat.

It was early morning when we reached the Plain of Reeds. The sun had just peaked into the sky. I heard the twin diesel engines reverse, striking me with the fear of the landing. A soft echo of prayers went through the hull of the boat and Sgt. Williams stood up. Everyone immediately followed his lead and smacked each other on the shoulders and helmets to try and break the thickness of anxiety. "Saddle up...lock and load," Sgt. Williams yelled out. The shoreline scraped the hull of the boat beneath our feet and with a sudden nudge the boat stopped. I watched the loading ramp lower and felt like a sardine trapped in a can and wanted more than anything to get out of the boat. I could see very little in front of me as we unloaded, just a stream of helmets dashing off the boat, men clanging in combat gear. I stepped onto dry land, my eyes quickly taking in the terrain before me.

There were few trees, mostly tall grass. I knelt down holding my gun with both hands, my finger softly resting on the trigger, ready to squeeze. My platoon formed a straight-line perimeter along the shore as the other platoons and companies unloaded. The high anxiety from the landing lowered inside of me and I took a deep breath of relief, lit a cigarette and watched the rest of Charlie Company unload. The gun boats, the Monitors and Alphas, seemed to hover in the water like crocodiles watching over their babies. It was a secure feeling having such fire power behind us, but I knew the further we moved away from the water, the less firepower they could back us up with.

Lt. Dimagard was in constant communication with the other platoon leaders and the company commander. We loved him. He had a charisma about himself, complimented by his good looks and athleticism. Lt. Dimagard's handlebar mustache and tall strong frame gave him the appearance of the perfect platoon leader. He was confirmed as our beloved leader the night Billy Don Kennington was killed. We saw him that night as one us, not some medal chasing officer trying to make a name for himself. We saw the frustration and sadness in him after losing one of his men. He was one of us—"the grunts" full of hopes and dreams like everyone else, fighting on the front lines for our country for freedom sake—and he believed in the cause.

The night we fought at the Cross Roads Lt. Dimagard held his composure, talking smoothly over the radio, even under a hail of enemy fire. I was often inside the CP because I was a medic and I knew him as well as anyone in our platoon.

Everything about him permeated leadership and although he demanded our obedience, without hesitation we followed him into combat. He had as much courage in combat as any man.

I stared at the near distant landscape in front of me. A few hundred feet away from the Landing Zone the terrain plummeted into a marsh of tall reed grass as far as I could see. Our straight line perimeter had loosely formed into a column and we began moving out into the Plain of Reeds following Tom's 1st squad. Even with the massive amount of American soldiers moving into the area with helicopters in the air, we seemed small compared to the vastness of the reeds. I watched the 1st Platoon drop into the marsh, disappearing into the 10 foot high grass as if the land itself was a beast, swallowing them whole.

After fifteen minutes I found myself up to my knees in mud and water and tall, sharp-edged, pale green grass stood tall over my head. I could see nothing but the GI's around me. The landscape was silent except muffled voices, radio chatter and sloshing mud. The mud squashed as I walked and made a sucking sound with every struggled pull of my legs. The smell of rotting vegetation was thick in the air. Roy Moseman once said,

"It was the worst place I had ever seen, nothing but tall grass and lots of canals and water. It was almost impossible to move in the area. It was canal after canal and tall, thick grass. The grass was as tall as we were and we couldn't see through it and we couldn't see over it."

The battalion commander was flying over the entire operation in a Cayuse helicopter, often breaking the radio silence. I had no idea where the other platoons were from our position, but I knew they were out there somewhere, maybe a kilometer away. It was like we were fighting the harsh terrain as much as the Viet Cong. The reeds themselves were sharp enough to cut open flesh. The Plain of Reeds was the perfect refuge for the enemy. The Viet Cong could be only a few feet away, hidden in the dense reeds, yet remain undetected.

Lt. Dimagard said we were falling behind and holding up the operation. His best defense was that we were standing in water up to our waist, spending more time helping eachother out of mud holes than we did moving forward. We had to meet at a rendezvous point with the rest of the battalion and until we reached our waypoint, the entire search and destroy operation slowed down to a crawl. Sgt. Williams tried to encourage us saying, "One more step closer to home boys," but the conditions were unsympathetic. My lunch consisted of a candy bar out of my pack while continuing the march through the mud and reeds.

Around mid morning we came to a canal, halting our progress even more. The terrain on the other side seemed somewhat dry and the reeds gave way to a sparse jungle. Lt. Dimagard was clearly annoyed with the situation. There were only two options—one was to wade across if our weapons could be held high enough above the water; or we could shoot a rope across with an M-79 grenade launcher. Sgt. Williams didn't like any of it, knowing our asses would be vulnerable and in the open. Lt. Dimagard and Sgt. Williams began to have a heated discussion about the area. Sgt. Williams didn't want to go another step forward. On the other side of the canal the reeds ended and dry open fields and tree lines dominated the landscape; it was the perfect place for an ambush.

The discussion ended. Lt. Dimagard talked with Overcast and then assumed the point position, walking directly toward the canal. Sgt. Williams gave the motion for us to follow and flank both sides. Lt. Dimagard knew we were uneasy with the posture of the land and as our leader, he headed toward the canal first. A few yards in front of me, he came to the edge of the brown water and checked the depth. He began to feel his way through the water and made a gesture letting us know it wasn't that deep.

After a few steps into the canal, Lt. Dimagard and Overcast were both blown back into the water by automatic gunfire from across the canal. Immediately the men around me returned fire, including Wilbanks on the M-60. Tunnel vision came to my eyes and I saw nothing but my platoon leader laying half out of the water and bullets pelleting the water around him. Within seconds, Tom and I grabbed him and pulled him into the cover of the tall reeds beside the shore. I noticed Overcast was hit in the abdomen, but had managed to crawl back into the cover of the grass. I turned my back to work on Lt. Dimagard and felt exposed to the enemy bullets cutting through the grass on all sides of me, but my platoon was shooting their asses off and I managed to control my fear.

I cut away Lt. Dimagard's shirt, noticing a single bullet hole through his left shoulder. "Your about to get the fuck out of here," I said to him as I checked his vitals. It looked like he smiled at me as a small trickle of blood streamed out of his mouth and down along his handlebar mustache. His pulse told me I was losing him and with frustration, I started giving him mouth to mouth, but with each breath I blew into him, I heard a sucking gurgling sound coming from somewhere on his body. I tore off his shirt, lifted his right arm and found an exit wound. The bullet ricocheted off his shoulder and passed through his chest, exiting under his arm. I looked at him again and realized his smile wasn't a smile, but was a grimace of pain. I tried and tried and tried and tried to resuscitate him, his blood all over my lips, but nothing worked.

In my exhaustion of breathing into him and beating on his chest, Roy Moseman had come over to help me, but clearly death was setting in. I had seen it too many times before and under the sounds of war, with his men shooting on either side of him, our adored leader, Lt. William Dimagard died in my arms. His last breath smelled of his last meal, barbeque beef. In the fifty years since the war has passed, it is a food I have never been able to eat.

I had no time to ponder the magnitude of the loss of such a man. The ambush raged on and I quickly turned toward Overcast who had been shot in the stomach. Swiftly, I put a dressing on his abdomen and pulled him back further into the security of the tall reeds. I began to regain my senses, learning that one of our squads had flanked and crossed the canal and was no longer pinned down, having taken out one of the enemy positions. The flanking squad had spotted one of the Viet Cong soldiers that possibly killed Lt. Dimagard and wounded Overcast hiding in a hole along the canal.

I sat next to Overcast and through the reeds watched our squad of men working their way along the canal. Richardson was on point and spotted the foxhole that harbored the enemy soldier. He slowly worked his way up toward the enemy position and without warning was shot in the chest, killing him instantly. Sgt. Williams had seen enough; he withdrew the squad from the area and called in air support. A Cayuse helicopter flew over, spotted the enemy position and circled back, unleashing several rockets into the hole, putting an end to the man that killed Lt. Dimagard.

We were still taking fire from the enemy as I helped Overcast move to a secure area for his evacuation. On our way to the LZ, artillery and airstrikes began to drop on the enemy positions, shaking the earth under my feet and sending black smoke ascending into the air behind us. As the shriek from the jets lowered, I noticed the enemy had finally been silenced. Normally I would feel relief, but the silence only made my thoughts of our loss more clear. A number of other GI's were with us as Overcast sat up leaning to one side, holding a cravat bandage on his stomach. The bullet entered to the right side of his belly button, but he was bleeding very little and the morphine had killed the pain.

We sat beside each other near the Landing Zone and talked about going home. The two of us had spent many nights smoking grass and drinking together and although happiness was nowhere to be found, I felt good that Overcast was going to make it. I had seen a few abdominal wounds by then and knew it was impossible to tourniquet an artery in such a place on the body—Overcast was lucky to be alive. The Dustoff chopper was in the distance and we popped smoke for the pilots, indicating the Landing Zone. When the chopper touched down, I helped Overcast and a couple other wounded GI's inside. The chopper lifted back into the sky and

Overcast waved with a pathetic smile, as if saying "Thanks."

We saddled up and crossed the canal. Since Richardson was on the other side of the canal, we floated Lt. Dimagard's body across the water on a small air raft. Williams and Moseman were the first to come upon Richardson's dead body. We all knew Sgt. Williams was good friends with him and that it hurt him real bad looking down at his body. Richardson was a neat guy, very talkative, always walking around with a tooth brush in his mouth. I pulled Richardson's personal belongings out of his pocket and his final letter to be sent home. After covering him with a poncho liner, we carried his body to Lt. Dimagard's near a clearing, where the helicopters would soon be landing.

The land was much dryer and sparse after crossing. We set up a small perimeter and secured the LZ. I sat on a dike beside Tom. In front of us were the body bags of Lt. Dimagard and Richardson and several dead Viet Cong. Just as we thought the area was secure, adrenaline raced through our hearts again as Tom and I watched a hat and the barrel of an AK-47 slowly rise out of a hole only yards away. The hat and the barrel of the gun slowly lowered back into the hole and we each grabbed grenades, pulled the pins, then tossed them in the hole. The explosion rocked the silence of the entire platoon. Sgt. Williams was yelling, "What the fuck's going on?" Tom reached in the hole and pulled out a mangled AK-47, his hands covered in blood and guts. He held it high in the air for everyone to see, like a souvenir—a reminder of completed vengeance of the day Lt. Dimagard and Richardson were killed.

I had washed a lot of blood from my hands while in Vietnam, but that day I remember vividly, kneeling beside the canal and smoking a cigarette with blood-stained hands. When I was done with my smoke, I rinsed the blood not only from my hands but also my face and lips. The death of Lt. William Dimagard struck a painful chord in us all. I can still see his face and remember the slight grin under his mustache while sitting inside the CP in the jungle or when he tried to be mad at us for joking around. I remember the horrific silence as we returned to the boats without him, each of us coming to grips with his death in our own way.

The name Dimagard means "God guard us." His brother Patrick once told me, half jokingly, "It didn't work all the time." He also told me a lot of things about their family such as their mother's best dishes, which were bacon and eggs on Sunday morning, and her fried chicken Sunday afternoons. They always went to 8:30 mass on Sunday morning and he and Bill would complain because their dad was an usher and they were always there by at least 8:00 am. Friday's during lent was a horror story, as their mother served an awful salmon patty. Usually

Bill and Patrick snuck up to Manner's for a Big Boy burger after dinner.

Patrick Dimagard sent me this E-mail:

"The last time I saw Bill was right after he graduated from OCS at Ft. Benning. He walked in my barracks to visit and he was wearing the blue ascot and blue helmet liner that all the graduates wore. He was very proud and I believe that he volunteered for Vietnam to utilize his infantry training. His birthday was March 31st and my parents arranged for everyone to send him cards for his 21st birthday. Unfortunately, he never made that date as he was killed on the 28th of March. All cards were returned to sender. Ralph Brickman, who was a prominent mortician in the Cleveland area, (also Bill's confirmation sponsor) was showing us available plots at All Souls Cemetery and during this procedure he could not contain himself and broke into an uncontrollable crying siege. The wake was held the day before Easter. So many people came that the wake was standing room only. This was at St. Paul's Euclid, where he and I attended grade school. Today, my mom, dad and Bill are now resting at All Souls Cemetery in Chardon, Ohio and there is a space reserved there for myself and wife, Suzanne."

Lt. Peter J. Cardello was the 3rd Platoon leader for Charlie Company; he had known Lt. Dimagard since they entered the service together. In a letter to Lt. Dimagard's parents he said, "You can be proud to have had a son like Bill who gave his life for his fellow men and his country in the cause of freedom—with honor. The men and officers of C-Company, 4th Battalion, 47th Infantry share your grief."

The last known photograph taken by Lieutenant William Dimagard of his 2nd Platoon before his death.

Lieutenant William Dimagard far right,
with his brother Patrick and his parents.

The Banana Grove

April 1968:

We returned to the Plain of Reeds once again, but this time it was on the outskirts with a much dryer approach and it was without Lt. Dimagard, Richardson and Overcast. Our new Lieutenant's last name was Dodds, a tall slender man, clean shaved, glasses and seemed to be a hard ass. He was green as green could be. By late afternoon we were inside a large body of jungle after taking on sniper fire all morning without incident. The sniper fire finally tapered down to nothing, but there was a tangible strangeness in the air, perhaps it was a logical fear inside me, telling me the land was too quiet. We knew the enemy was in the area and would only attack if the odds were in their favor.

As darkness shrouded us, a perimeter and CP was set up for the night. Three squads were placed on the edge of a grass field overlooking about two hundred yards of dry rice field. Beyond the field was a large jungle. On both sides of us were sparse jungles that almost looked like fields, but were slowly being overtaken by sporadic tangles of palm trees.

The Command Post was placed about fifty yards behind the center squad and two other squads were placed on either side it. Behind us was the thick jungle we had just cut through having made no contact with the enemy. I recall there was another platoon somewhere to the rear of our position, allowing us to focus on the front and sides of the perimeter. Our perimeter made up a part of a much larger perimeter, but we were still far from being shoulder to shoulder with the other platoons.

It was dusk as I heard the whapping of the re-supply chopper. Sgt. Williams sat next to me on the radio, telling the pilots what color we would "pop smoke." It could be a number of different colors— violet, yellow, orange and red. Having different colored smoke prevented the Viet Cong from popping smoke of the same color and drawing choppers into an ambush. As the chopper flew in, the rotor wash from the blades blew down the grass and twisted the colored smoke in the air like a tornado. Along with a few others I began running toward the chopper, but gunfire opened up on us from the distant jungle. Bullets zipped over our heads and began pelting the hell out of the helicopter. The Viet Cong had opened up on the chopper from the main jungle. The pilots pulled their chopper out of the Landing Zone and when it left the area, the firing stopped. Artillery began dropping on the enemy position, turning the distant jungle into a burning rubbish pile.

It was dark when the re-supply flew in for the second attempt, but before the helicopter made it to our LZ, the enemy opened up from a different position, crippling the chopper, sending it back to Dong Tam before we could get resupplied.

As strange as it was, a Viet Cong soldier stood up somewhere in the field and opened up on our position, sending green tracers shrieking over our heads. We opened up with everything we had, including Wilbanks on the M-60. When we stopped firing, the Viet Cong stood up and fired again. We returned fire a second time, but this time puzzled, wondering how the hell we missed him or whoever was in the field the first time. Tom swore he had his sights right dead on his body.

Sgt. Williams called in illumination rounds to light up the field, but we could see nothing. Gunfire opened up on us again from in the middle of the field and we returned fire toward the silhouette of an enemy soldier. Sgt. Williams started screaming over the sound of automatic weapons fire, "Hold your fire, hold your fucking fire," and the firing ceased. I couldn't believe we never hit the Viet Cong soldier. Sgt. Williams then realized the Viet Cong were trying to drain us of ammunition by drawing our fire. The enemy was crude, knowing full well our re-supply chopper never dropped its load. We were already low on ammo to begin with and by then we were almost out.

Word was a re-supply chopper was inbound and was going to make the drop somewhere at the rear of our platoon, but I couldn't hear any helicopters at the time. Each squad had a starlight scope to help identify objects at night. Tom's squad was on the edge of the grass field, overlooking the rice field that led into dense jungle where the ambush was launched at the first re-supply attempt. They were center, with a squad on each side of them about sixty yards away. I was struck with fear when all three squads reported movement through their starlight scopes. The radio turned alive, "Beaucoup movement in the tree line, Charlie's all over the fucking place," one of the squads reported back. I left the CP and moved to Tom's position and watched the enemy, waiting in a thick fear, knowing we were low on ammunition.

The first squad was where the tree line met the grass field and it was a bad place to be. For several long minutes we watched the enemy moving in the jungle a couple hundred yards away and suddenly the distance erupted with gunfire and the sky lit up with the enemy's green tracers. The Viet Cong advanced at a fast pace with guns ablaze, creeping all over the place, down our flanks and even in the open field directly in front of us. I returned fire next to Tom and Wilbanks. It was chaos, with only two choices—run or hide. We made the decision to hide knowing it was too late to do anything else. It was the greatest fear I had ever felt in my life. Tom and I tucked ourselves behind a dike and listened to the 1st squad screaming in combat, fighting for their lives.

Green and red tracers zipped over our heads and hit the earth beside me. Human shadows raced over top of us, stepping off the dike we hid behind. Tom and I made the decision to get the hell out of there before they found us and on our bellies we crawled toward the banana grove that we had spotted on the way into the grass field. I was on Tom's heels with tracer rounds both red and green flying over our heads. The voices of Viet Cong were everywhere, screaming as they shot toward our platoon that we were separated from. I was so close to Tom as we crawled my hands often hit his ankles. We finally reached the edge of the banana grove, our chest's pumping air and our eyes wide with fear.

We weren't very far from our platoon, but we were afraid to move. After a few moments of rest we heard Viet Cong talking and we moved deeper into the banana grove. The grove had several rows of trees and between the trees were ditches, filled with three feet of water. We gently slid down into one of the ditches, painfully slow, fearful the enemy would hear us. The shooting had stopped, but strange Vietnamese voices were all around us. Tom and I kind of half stood in the ditch, our bodies resting on the mud bank, looking at each other with shock in our eyes.

After several hours of hiding in the banana grove, we heard Vietnamese voices coming toward us, quickly closing in on our position. A squad of Viet Cong made a half circle around us and stopped about thirty yards in front of us. They made a smoldering campfire that told us we must have been well inside their perimeter. There were six of them with AK-47's and one machine gun. Unlike the NVA soldiers that dressed similar to us, they were Guerilla fighters in black pajamas and khaki-colored clothes.

Typical uniforms worn by Vietcong Guerilla fighters with AK-47 assault rifles.

I looked at Tom and we both realized the firelight was reflecting off our faces. We took mud from the ditch and smeared it on our faces. The Viet Cong smoked cigarettes and drank whiskey, laughing at jokes all night long and I even think they may have been smoking marijuana before they put out the fire and went to sleep. The funny thing about that night is, more than anything, I remember looking at Tom and pointing at my pack of smokes; we wanted a cigarette so bad.

The Viet Cong moved out before daylight and we stayed in the ditch and listened to a silent jungle while leeches sucked on our bodies. At dawn we slipped a tiny bit further out of the ditch and looked for signs of the enemy, but saw nothing. We couldn't see fifty feet through a thick fog hanging low under the treetops. It was like a savior had come when, all at once, the sun came up and helicopters began circling the area. High above the Cayuse and Huey choppers, two Huey Cobras were ready to come down and unleash their guns and rockets.

Tom had a compass and map to help us move toward the area we swept through the day before, but we had a good idea were our platoon was anyways. We took one last slow look from inside the ditch and then quietly slipped out of the banana grove and were on the move. It wasn't long before we saw American soldiers policing the area for dead and wounded Viet Cong and GI's. We didn't exchange too many words with the unknown American soldiers, except a slow nod of the head and "What a fucking night, huh?" On the way back I looked over at Tom's tall lanky body and noticed blood from the leeches he had ripped off and I gestured for him to wipe his face.

We met back up with our platoon and we were all disorganized, as if someone shook us up in a shaker. We were cranked up and talking out of control. "Did you see that fuck'n this and that fuck'n that?" was all I heard. The Army flew in breakfast and we ate cold eggs, toast and bacon. None of us had slept or ate, but we were all wide awake, feeling good to be alive.

As it turned out, the squad that was overran to the left of my position lost two men. Although we hated losing men, they were new to the platoon, and after losing Lt. Dimagard and Richardson, the veterans in the platoon didn't say much of the loss. After eating, the airlift came in kicking up dust and bending the grass. The choppers set down before us and it was the love-hate relationship again—the sound of the choppers one of love this time. The popping helicopter told us we were on our way back to the safe confines of Dong Tam.

Doc MacSwan in flight

A Hunting We Will Go

The horror of war had escalated and no one really thought they would make it home in one piece. We were not only physically drained from the harsh terrain of the Plain of Reeds, but we were emotionally drained as well. I was still fighting inner emotions after the death of Lt. Dimagard. The veterans in my platoon were Ting, Tom Ziehm, Roy Moseman, Garvy, Roscoe Knowlin, Wilbanks, Washington, Freeman and Sgt. Williams. Sgt. Maynard was transferred to a headquarters unit shortly after the death of Lt Dimagard and Richardson. Every one of us had seen enough death, but Vietnam kept dishing it out.

We had become as close as men could be and easily identified each other in pitch darkness by recognizing the silhouettes of each other. We truly became brothers. We almost felt sorry for the new guys coming in, but we protected our emotions by being apprehensive of forming new friendships. We had lost enough friends and seen enough death, yet it still would not end. Things had heated up quite a bit in the delta and we were being shipped out on missions almost every day. Contact with the enemy was no longer an "if," it was "when and where?"

Roscoe Nowlin should have never been allowed in Vietnam. He had an innocence about him, a child like mentality - always scared and talking wild. His mother once wrote him a letter, telling him his turtle had died and she used it for soup. He cried for days after reading the letter.

We loved him in a big brother kind of way, always making sure he didn't do something stupid. He was horrible at throwing hand grenades, so nobody let him carry any, fearing he might kill himself or one of us. Something in him wasn't right, but we sure watched over him. Roscoe was as much a part of our brotherhood as anyone, but he sure didn't belong in the Nam. On several occasions he stood up during a firefight and we had to tackle him, slapping him in the face to calm him down. After everything we had been through, if there were guardian angels in Vietnam, they were sure as shit keeping an eye on Roscoe.

Roy Moseman reminded me years after the war about a mission we were on with Roscoe. Roy went on to say:

"We were walking in a banana grove. The Vietnamese would dig rows of canals with strips of land about 15 feet wide in between the canals. It was terrible to walk in because we had to get in the canal and climb back out. We had to do this repeatedly and it wore our ass out. We had just moved across several of these canals when the VC started shooting at us. It was just about dark and not a good time to get into a firefight.

I heard a guy scream. He had been hit by small arms fire. I think he was from another platoon, because I don't remember his name or anything else about him. Just about that time, the Viet Cong fired a B-40 rocket and it actually grazed Roscoe Nowlin on the arm and then hit the mud beside him. It didn't explode. Roscoe grabbed Tony Garvy around the neck and screamed, "Pray for us Garvy, we are going to die." Only Roscoe Clyde Nowlin could be lucky enough to get hit by a B-40 rocket and live to tell about it."

The next mission I can remember started when we were staying on the birthing ship the USS Appleton. We just called it the "Apple." I was playing cards with Ting and some of the guys when Sgt. Williams busted in saying, "Saddle up boys... Tango boats are waiting." We all looked at each other in shock because we were supposed to be on stand down, but nobody was about to argue with Sgt. Williams.

The Tango boats took us to Dong Tam. As it turned out, the enemy had been spotted and a sister company needed us as a blocking force. We unloaded in the harbor and were trucked to the tarmac. We formed up and the helicopters were ready to go with the door gunners half resting on their machine guns. I was in Sgt. William's chopper along with Ting and several others. Lt. Dodds sat where Dimagard had once sat and put on the radio helmet.

In a big, sweeping loud roar, we lifted into the air. When we lifted out of Dong Tam, the riverine troops were already underway. The Riverine Force had the job of executing the sweeping operation and we, as the airmobile, would act as the blocking force. It was like a classic deer drive, which many of the grunts were familiar with. Special forces or spotter planes often located the enemy prior to operations and once the enemy was detected, they could be flushed out, blocked off, and decimated.

The Army wasn't holding anything back that day. The rice field and the wildlife surrounding it were silent that hot morning and the leaves were without a ripple in the stagnant air. Like a lightning bolt shooting through the sky, we entered the silent land with our machines, flying low, nearly touching the treetops. I always feared landing in open fields, where we were the most vulnerable with no cover. Seconds before unloading, the door gunners leaned heavy on their guns and we pulled our helmets out from under our asses and put them on our heads. It was a moment of both fear and also power. The fear was of death and the power was similar to that of Hitler's Blitzkrieg, knowing as we landed we were the most powerful element on the battlefield. We quickly unloaded and formed a perimeter inside the treeline, facing the suspected approach of the enemy.

We waited inside the trees for about 30 minutes until the silence was broken by the lift of helicopters landing a few hundred yards away to our left, dropping off the rest of our company. My platoon quickly formed up and began humping through the brush. We were moving at a pretty good speed. I thought someone sure as hell knew where we were going.

I felt fear, as with any other mission, but in Vietnam fear wasn't some kind of cancerous emotion, it was just there. Fear was in the air that we breathed. For the infantry soldier in Vietnam, fear was similar to a civilian's pet dog or a cat—it's always around, running and playing with your mind, chasing after you, wanting to be loved. Fear had to be embraced; it was constant.

I continued taking one step after another in a land cloaked in booby traps, my eyes intent on the surrounding brush. Something as simple as a bird rustling in a nest brought my entire being to full alert. In the jungle, relaxation wasn't part of the equation; to actually relax would bring on certain injury or death. While on a mission relaxation was anything but combat. We were always alert, our gun barrels moving with our eyes.

We landed in the rice field without incident. Beyond the field was dense jungle with a few small clearings about seventy yards away. There was a small hooch on the tree line, probably used by farmers that needed a break from the sun or for mothers to feed their children in the shade. It was also the perfect place for Wilbanks to set up his M-60 machine gun.

I went inside the hooch with Tom and Wilbanks. Our platoon spread out through the tree line, along with the rest of the company. We watched one platoon slipping and struggling their way across the rice field a few hundred yards to the left of our position. I began to take in the jungle across the small field, searching for enemy movement. We started eating lunch, bringing our food to our mouths, still watching for movement. In the distance we heard gunfire as another battalion made contact a long ways away from our position. The chatter over the radio turned alive.

We listened to the firefight for what seemed an hour and suddenly, everyone at the same time saw movement in the jungle across the field. We struggled to see if they were American GI's. Sgt. Williams got on the radio and asked the other platoons to pop smoke and when they did, we realized they were nowhere near us. As the unknown soldiers hit a small clearing it became obvious the Viet Cong were trying to sneak out the back door. Shooting across the field, our tree line erupted with fire. The three of us shot from inside the hooch, like shooting fish in a barrel. There were dozens of enemy soldiers scurrying along the edge of the jungle. Some made it through, but many dropped in the clearing. They continued to run through the clearing into the jungle making it a lot harder for us to hit them, but we continued assaulting the jungle with hundreds of rounds of ammunition.

Fleeing our bursts of automatic gunfire, the Viet Cong formed a position several hundred yards across the field to our left, running smack dab into the 1st Platoon igniting a furious firefight. As the Viet Cong tried to fight their way out of entrapment, even more of the enemy soldiers flooded into the area. But they were out of our range, stacking up near the crippled 1st Platoon like cars in a traffic jam. It was clear the enemy had to make a final stand, having been pushed all over the map trying to make an exit from the battlefield.

Unluckily, about ten men from the 1st Platoon were still stuck in the field, pinned down behind a mud dike near the edge of the jungle. Inside the jungle about 200 yards away, the rest of the platoon was holding their own, fighting for their lives, pouring down coverfire for our brothers in the rice field. I felt helpless, intently watching as bullets continuously streamed over the heads of the men and into the mud dike they hid behind. I had seen it all before, men unable to move or shoot back as the wounded lay motionless, only yards away from the enemy, praying for a savior.

Our new platoon leader was obviously shaken, barely able to speak into the radio, but made the smartest decision he could by relying on Sgt. William's advice. Without hesitation, they quickly ordered me to go with Tom's first squad to slip back and then down the tree line within range of the enemy and help free up the men caught in the field. We left the hooch, unnoticed by the enemy deep inside the cover of the jungle, and moved toward the firefight.

At first we could only hear the steady fire of the enemy's AK-47's. After moving about 100 yards, we crept toward the field and nearly on top of the 1st Platoon, where we could see the enemy. We were all they had for a savior since dropping artillery rounds and air-strikes could easily kill everyone. Immediately, we picked our targets and unleashed our weapons, including several M-79 grenade launchers. Wilbank's machine gun quickly caught the attention of the VC and we came under fire, but it was enough for the men in the field to pop their heads up and return fire. We helped turn the tables and it was the enemy now fighting for their lives, falling back further into the jungle away from us. Although out of sight, the firefight raged on inside the distant jungle, As it turned out we managed to create some space between the 1ˢᵗ Platoon and the enemy and that was all they needed, just a little space, to bring a sudden end to the battle.

The Viet Cong must have known their time was up. As the shooting and the radio revealed the intensity of the fighting, the Viet Cong became suicidal, deliberately and directly running into the 1st Platoon's perimeter. The words, "Fire for effect" rang out over the radio and moments later, whistling in from behind us, artillery shells began exploding on the enemy position, toppling the trees and drowning the enemy with an unimaginable helpless terror. Within minutes after the barrage of artillery ended, F-4 Phantom jets shrieked in low from behind us with a deafening noise. I watched the jets fly over the enemy and circle back behind us. As the F-4's flew in again they released High Explosive (HE) bombs or "Willy Pepper" as we called it.   Before the remaining enemy could breathe, the bombs whistled in a few feet over our heads and detonated, shaking the earth with a quake and turning the jungle in front of us into a blazing inferno.

Two more F-4 Phantoms immediately followed and screamed in over our heads, releasing bombs filled with white phosphorous, which was able to burn through clothing and flesh straight to the bone within minutes. Seconds after the phosphorus bombs burst in the air; Wilbanks started screaming about ten yards away from me. Instantly I realized some of the splashing jelly-like phosphorous had landed on the back of his neck. I ran to him, cut off the back of his shirt and noticed a hole burning into his neck the size of my thumb. Knowing white phosphorous needed oxygen to burn, I quickly packed the hole with mud, covered the wound with plastic and gave him a little bit of morphine. The firefight was over and with one arm around Wilbanks, I looked at the tree line in awe. There was nothing left alive, even the jungle itself was dead and burning. We had created another moonscape of bomb craters, killing perhaps hundreds of the Viet Cong.

We airlifted out the wounded and I slapped Wilbanks on the chest and said good-bye. After the medical evacuation we "cleaned up our frags" and "left nothing for the dinks," which meant all of our brass bullet casings and C-Ration cans or anything else the enemy could use against us. Something as simple as a tin can could be used as a deadly booby trap. As we policed the area, we found an unexploded bomb near the edge of the devastated jungle where the enemy was trying to fight for their lives. My platoon formed a perimeter around the dud bomb and waited for an Explosive Ordinance Disposal (EOD) unit to come in and remove it.

After sitting around, smoking cigarettes and talking about how we kicked some Viet Cong ass, EOD showed up, rigged the bomb with a harness and lifted it with a helicopter out of the area. As our airlift picked us up another infantry company stayed behind to tally up a body count and throw the dead into the bomb craters. It was one of the most perfectly executed missions I remember, having trapped and killed so many Viet Cong and with us taking so few casualties. As my helicopter left the battlefield, I couldn't help but look down at the trash pile we left. It was an awesome sight.

The Tango's took us back to our ship after landing in Dong Tam. Ting was still there with a drunken smile after kicking everyone's ass in poker. New faces were coming in every day and I just looked at them with pity. They had not a single clue what we had been through, nor did they know of the hell that awaited them. After seeing my original platoon get so decimated, the drunken laughs over the card table seemed more false than ever. Everyone seemed to talk a little less. I thought about home a little more.

It was hard, always having a new guy coming up and asking a million questions. I usually said, "Just keep your ass down GI." We called the new guys FNG's (fucking new guys)—and we more commonly called them "Cherries." The cherry was ultimately popped after their first time in combat and they wouldn't have a very long wait.

DUSTOFF 82

The monsoon rain fell like the tears of God. The Mekong was like a wet sponge and our rules of engagement were simple—if someone knocked on the door, shoot through the door and then answer it. New faces filled the ranks of Charlie Company, replacing the dead and wounded. I felt as if I had been spit there, dropped into a land of mud. The mud and water were like quicksand and it was everywhere. The heat was unforgivably hot and humid.

I talked to God every day using simple words, but I meant every word I said. A man cannot be more sincere with God, than when he is preparing for death. I asked God to watch over me and left my hope for life in his hands. Sure I still felt fear, but I remember thinking, "If it's my time, it's my time." It was a dangerous mentality to have.

Sgt. Williams notified everyone that we would be pulling a search and destroy operation in the morning. Like every other mission, I didn't like it, but tried not to think about it the night before. There were other things to think about. Things like going home. What it would be like? What would people say? I finished up the night with one last cigarette, wrote a letter home to my wife and said a prayer.

April 24, 1968:

We loaded the Tango boats early the next morning. It was my first mission without Tom Ziehm. I remember it being odd without him there. We had become inseparable, forming a closeness I can hardly describe. If I looked left or right, Tom was always on one of them. The only time we weren't together was when Tom was on point, and I heard him do plenty of bitching about that.

Tom's jungle rot had pestered him for a long time. I always carried extra socks for him, but the Mekong Delta never gave Tom's feet and legs a chance to heal and the fungus eventually left open wounds and scars and showed signs of infection. Tom's jungle rot had become so bad that the "lucky son of a bitch" was working laundry on the USS Colleton. Although Tom and I were inseparable, it was always good to see a buddy get out of combat alive and well.

I sat in a Tango boat in the same fashion as any other mission. I didn't read from my white Bible anymore. I knew every single phrase by heart, but I still had it neatly placed in the front of my helmet.

We landed without any contact from the Viet Cong near an ancient farming village. It was hot as usual, but at least we were given the treat of walking on dry ground for a change. Nothing was more tiring then trudging through canals, ditches and banana groves, which is what we were in more often than not. We were cautious as we approached the village. Farmers and villagers could see us coming a mile away. A guerilla fighter would have had plenty of time to set down his farming hoe, set up a booby trap and resume his work before we arrived. We couldn't trust anyone. It was not uncommon to roll over a dead Viet Cong after a firefight and see the lifeless face of a woman.

It didn't take us long to reach a small village of straw hooches and we started to search the area for signs of the enemy. We didn't have to look very hard. We immediately found communication wire running through all of the hooches and into the surrounding jungle. We began checking identification badges, turning the quiet village into a roar of crying Vietnamese as they pled about their innocence. We found enough rice to feed a large unit of Viet Cong. Some of the men in my platoon interrogated people, others searched the village and as always, there was a squad pulling security, watching for an attack.

Everyone we checked out had the proper identification, which sent a chill down my spine, knowing somewhere around us the Viet Cong had melted back into the jungle, most likely watching our every move. When we were getting ready to move out again, the bunkers and extra food were blown with hand grenades and the few suspected Viet Cong were tied together with a rope and flown out. Ever since that little girl with the headless doll, I made time for the children. I found myself emotionally sensitized to only the children and desensitized to the dead. The dead no longer suffered. As the adults, both men and women were guilty in my mind.

We moved out of the village through an uncommonly dry rice field. The field was still muddy, but we weren't up to our waist in the shit. Everyone was talking loud and shooting comments back and forth, knowing for certain we weren't going to surprise the enemy that day. We knew if the Viet Cong were in the area, they were already watching.

While leaving the burning village a Riverine Force was unloading on our right flank. It gave us a little bit of comfort, knowing we weren't the only company in the area. As the village grew more and more distant, a haunting tree line of dense jungle became clear. We became quiet and started using our eyes more intently. I had been carrying a balsa wood stump tied around my ass so I had something to sit on during our breaks, but as we neared the chilling jungle, all horseplay stopped and I cut the stump from my body, leaving it to rot in the rice field.

The mission had gone smooth, but when we left the village, we knew the enemy was in the area. Nobody seemed too concerned until we neared the tree line. We were about seventy yards away from its edge when the silence was shattered. The tree line opened up with enemy fire. I hit the dirt as fast as I could and crawled forward, taking cover behind a dike. I took a quick glance making sure nobody was wounded and without a specific target, I returned fire back into the jungle. Within seconds the enemy was shooting at me and I slipped my head back down behind the dike. They were putting it on us pretty good with a steady stream of bullets pelting our position. The enemy fire slowed down, but the second we tried to raise our heads and shoot back, the enemy let loose a fury of automatic gunfire. After we buried our heads into the mud again, the enemy fire returned to almost nothing.

After realizing we weren't getting out of the field any time soon, I rolled over on my back to look up at the sky, wondering how long the enemy was going to stick around this time. For the Viet Cong to be so brave, knowing our air-support capabilities, I figured they must have been dug in well, hiding in bunkers. As funny as it may seem, I opened up my flack jacket and tried to even out my tan. I remember big white puffy clouds, blue sky and in the far distance, a dense black monsoon rain lingering. For a brief moment hell broke loose again and then lowered, but they still had us pinned down.

We called for artillery support and the rounds started coming in and pounding the earth seventy yards in front of us. I think we were getting as much shrapnel as the enemy because the ground was dry, allowing the exploding shell fragments to travel much further. When the artillery explosions stopped we returned fire, but the enemy quickly let us know they were unaffected by cannon fire. Several minutes went by and another barrage of artillery hit the jungle. We returned fire as the shells were exploding and the enemy matched us bullet for bullet.

Striking me with an all too familiar dread, I heard the shout "Medic" echo under the sounds of combat. I looked over and saw Roy Moseman holding his arm. I didn't feel like crawling on my belly, so I half stood and bolted into a scooting run with hell continuing to break loose. I scooted as fast as I could with Moseman the only man inside my tunnel vision. I was a few feet away from Moseman and was thrown through the air into a spin. It felt like I had been cracked across my leg with a willow branch, but it wasn't going away. From the momentum of running, when I fell to the earth I slid, landing right next to Roy Moseman. Then I thought in a brief second, "I can't believe I'm hit." My entire groin and ass became numb with a stinging sensation and I reached down and felt the back of my leg. I felt warm blood saturating my pants and I couldn't tell where I had been hit.

Shlogal crawled over to me and I began looking at Moseman's arm. Luckily, the shrapnel that hit his forearm didn't break any bones. I gave him a pressure dressing while Shlogal was on his elbows cutting off my pant leg. I asked him, "How bad is it?" He replied with an answer I didn't want to hear, "I can't tell you're bleeding too much." I thought I might have been hit in the testicles. I reached down with a bloody hand and made sure everything was still there and it was. Shlogal helped me tourniquet my leg, with some sort of stick, so I could release blood and keep my leg alive.

We weren't far from Dong Tam and I could already hear the Dustoff on the way. Sgt. Williams yelled with a radio in his hand, "They're coming down one time...one time only." Moseman and I made a break for the LZ back toward the village. Several others had also been wounded, but I don't recall who they were. I never ran so hard in my life. I uttered the words while I ran, "Get me the fuck out of here." There was a wide ditch we had to cross and it seemed like it was twenty feet wide. I swear I set some sort of Olympic jump record. I knew the enemy was shooting at Moseman and I and the chopper we were running to, but all I remember is that beyond the ditch was my savior, the descending chopper. I leapt with all the strength in my body, landing on the other side, never even touching the water. It seemed within seconds the helicopter was before me and I slid into the chopper on my belly like a baseball slide. I looked down at my leg and noticed the tourniquet was around my ankles doing absolutely nothing and blood was all over the fucking place. The Dustoff lifted into the air and the medic on board started placing a real tourniquet on my leg. Moseman and I glanced down at the battlefield with a similar stare with bullets zipping through the air around us and pinging off the helicopter. What a feeling that was!

We landed on the USS Colleton and medical personnel quickly rushed us into surgery. The entire back of my leg was ripped open. My skin looked like a mouth agape, two inches wide. Come to find out, my bloody clothes were sent below deck, where Tom was working. He picked up the blood and mud stained clothes and read the words MacSwan. He thought I was killed.

I was lying on my belly cursing at the pain as the nurses poked local anesthetic needles around the wound in my leg. Tom rushed into the operating room, and said, "Doc, I thought you were dead." I looked up, remembering it was my first mission without Tom, I replied, "Mother fucker it's all your fault." I tried to smile at Tom, but the pain overwhelmed me as the surgeon began cutting dead tissue and nerves. My cursing and screaming came to a complete stop as if God himself numbed me, when I noticed a Rock Tiger from the ARVN special forces, smoking a cigarette with a tourniquet on his arm that ended above the elbow. He was calm as could be and the sight of him silenced me. I realized how lucky I was. I was still in pain, but somehow managed to internalize it, while feeling the eyes of the armless man watching me. They stitched up the tissue on the inner part of my wound and left some of the meat flapped open, allowing them to flush it out to prevent infection. Roy Moseman was going through the same shit in another room, but I figured he was going to be fine.

After surgery Tom came in to see me. My wife Marsha had mailed a box of cookies that we ate as we listened to our company fight the Viet Cong all night over the radio. We thought about saving some cookies for the guys after a night in hell, but they were too good and we ate the whole box. Jokingly, I assured Tom I didn't blame him for me getting wounded.

I spent three days with an open wound on crutches. The male nurses flushed out the hole in my leg several times a day. I spent a lot of time with Tom, sharing some of our most intimate fears and thoughts. I knew Tom was going home soon and I listened to him talk about deer hunting and fishing back in Michigan. After three days, the medical personnel were convinced there was no infection and the surgeon brought me back in to stitch my leg up. The skin on the back of my leg was dried and tight and when they prodded the area again with needles, I felt the greatest pain ever in my life. I cursed and screamed once again, but this time I think I made up a few new curse words. They held me down as the surgeon pulled the two tightly receded flaps of skin back together for the final stitching. If they hadn't held me down, I swear I would have been throwing punches. After one hundred and eighty stitches, I was finished.

After spending a week in recovery the Army gave me transfer orders back to my same company, but this time I was going to the 4th Mortar Platoon. When I read the orders I felt sick to my stomach. I thought I had earned a ticket out of the field, but medics weren't lasting long and were in short supply. My days of combat were not over yet.

Little Green Apples

After two weeks of recovery, I flew to Hawaii and met my wife. We spent a few days together, but I felt distant from the civilization around me, as if I didn't belong. My feet had walked on a blood stained earth of screaming men, women and children, and now they stepped in sand on the shores of a tourist's paradise with my leg still recovering from my wounds. I loved my wife and it was great to see her, but I knew Vietnam awaited me once again. I left the Hawaiian Islands with a lump in my throat, wanting so badly to go back to the farm with my wife.

I flew back into Vietnam and landed at an airstrip near Bearcat. I met up with Les McKenzie, who I knew from boot camp. I hadn't seen him since he was working in the hospital, the same night Garcia got hit during the Tet offensive. We spent three days together drinking at Les's barracks and at a patio bar not far away. At the end of the three days, I was already two days late returning to duty. Luckily, it wasn't hard to find a chopper flying into Dong Tam. With the pilot relaying over the radio my name on board, the military police were waiting for me when we landed.

The police escorted me to my company commander Captain Brown, and knowing he was a hardened combat soldier, I had an enormous amount of respect for the man. He was furious with me, saying, "MacSwan you've been AWOL for three days...your lucky I don't Article 15 your ass." I didn't say a single word and stood at attention. The captain then paused, gesturing to me - he wanted a verbal response for my actions. I replied "What are you gonna do...put me in combat?" I was thinking, "I'll take a jail cell hospital over the jungle any day.' Captain Brown knew who I was, having pinned me with my medals. He was with us at the Plain of Reeds, the day his fellow officer Lt. Dimagard died in my arms. A half smirk came over his face and he said with a low grumble, "MacSwan...get the fuck out of here and get back to your platoon."

The 4th Mortar Platoon provided close artillery support for the 1st, 2nd and 3rd Platoons. Since my battalion, the 4th and 47th was on riverine operations my orders were to report to a 4-Deuce mortar barge in the Dong Tam harbor. I didn't think I would know anyone and was happy to find Ed Padden from my old platoon there. He was not only from my old platoon, but also grew up near my hometown. Before he was wounded during the Tet Offensive, he and I had spent many nights talking about life in Western New York, and a small rowdy bar we both knew by the name, "The Marlboro Inn."

The barge itself was clearly made for combat. It was olive drab, rectangular in shape and the midsection was elevated giving the average-sized man plenty of height to stand. On top of the midsection was a 50 cal. machine gun, surrounded by a 2 foot wall of sandbags, but the chief weapons aboard were the 4-Deuce mortars placed on each end of the barge. Underneath the machine gun deck were two rooms: the bunk area, enough to sleep eight men, with a large round table bolted to the floor; and another room, steel plated on all walls, with a coordinates table and a blown up map of Ding Tong and other surrounding provinces.

Soon after I boarded the barge Tom came to say good-bye. The jungle rot finally gave him a ticket home. We didn't exchange very many words and it was quiet, mostly we just stared at each another with grins. We hugged and with a slap on the back, Tom left for the states. I watched his tall, strong, lanky frame swagger out of sight. His rubber Superman figure was no longer in his helmet, nor was it in mine and Bruce (Moose) Johnson probably didn't have his either. As Tom walked away I felt a very real void enter inside me, but as much as I loved him, it was good to see him make it home in one piece.

The crew on the barge was Sgt. Owens, Sgt. Sandy Frost, Sgt. Pounds, Ed Padden, Richardson, Joe Capitano, Chester Goloski, Tex and myself. The first week on the barge was boring, but it was a boredom I embraced, writing letters to home, playing cards, and making trips to the PX for shaving supplies, shampoo and cigarettes. We spent the nights drinking in Dong Tam or sitting on top of the barge next to the 50 cal. machine gun, listening to records and smoking grass. The veterans on the barge told me to enjoy the down time and assured me it wasn't always so quiet.

Sandy Frost was a likable guy, with light hair and a slender body. He always had his dog "Hombre" by his side. Having a dog running around, begging for food, playing, barking and cuddling with us brought the nostalgia of home to our barge. Although I missed my brothers in the 2nd Platoon, it was a good crew of guys. On top of it all, I knew there would be no more trudging in the jungle through mud and water.

One night, soon after I reported to the mortar platoon, we were docked in the Dong Tam harbor and our generator ran out of oil and quit running. Our major concern was getting the lights back on for our poker games. As we stumbled through the darkness, we came up with the idea to find another generator. The huge demand for oil at the time made it much easier to find a generator than oil, especially in the middle of the night, and with a brilliant plan in place we left the barge in search of a generator.

On the road that ran along the harbor, a Jeep was parked in the shadows. Knowing the Jeeps in Dong Tam could be easily started by a toggle switch—with or without a key, drunk as skunks, Cappy, Chester Goloski and I loaded into the Jeep. Cappy got behind the wheel and quickly started the engine. According to plan, we drove a short distance to the back of the nurse's barracks that was lined with generators. Under the black of night, we staggered up to one of the generators, picked it up and carried it back to the Jeep.

After the short drive to the barge, we parked at the end of the floating pier, unloaded the generator and carried it to the side of the barge. Seconds after wrestling the generator aboard, headlights warned us of an approaching vehicle. Without hesitating we dumped the stolen generator into the harbor. As the lights drew closer we panicked, noticing the stolen Jeep parked cock-eyed at the end of our pier. I led the charge to the Jeep, put it in neutral and we rolled it into the water.

The headlights shined on us bright, stopping at the end of the pier, illuminating us as we stood smoking cigarettes. Two military police stepped out and walked down to us, the water still gurgled as the Jeep sank to the bottom of the harbor. Luckily

Dong Tam was not a quiet place and the police walked by the bubbles in the water and stopped a short distance away from us. With the bright lights shining on us, we couldn't make out even the smallest amount of their appearance, but we knew they were eyeballing every one of us.

After a statement about the missing generator, followed by a question as to where we had been that night, I assured them we played cards all night and were smoking our last cigarettes before hitting the racks. My response satisfied their curiosity and they quickly turned around, got in their jeep and left the area. We decided to go without lights for the night and request a new generator in the morning. I finished the night with the guys on top of the barge, all of us circled around the 50 caliber machine gun, leaning against sandbags, listening to music and smoking marijuana.

A few days after we were issued our new generator, we received orders for a mission and I overheard Sgt. Owens talking about his need for a Vietnamese interpreter on the barge. Immediately I recalled the day Tom left and him telling me Ting had been wounded with shrapnel, but was healing up well. With approval from Sgt. Owens, I went to Ting's home just outside the Dong Tam perimeter. I was excited to see my old buddy, having not seen him since the day I was wounded.

As I neared Ting's home, I recalled the countless times he saved us by spotting booby traps.

He was such a joker, often with a giddy child-like personality, but out in the jungle he was shrewdly intelligent, finding traps hidden under leaves and grenades strung through the trees. Many times in combat, Ting knew the Viet Cong's next move before they made it. He loved Americans and, after saving our lives, we couldn't help but love him as a brother.

When he saw me, Ting shouted out my name with a smile on his face. We hugged, sat down and had a few shots of rice whiskey together, talking about the old. A long fresh scar was healing on the left side of his face. He kept looking at me, saying with his broken English, "I miss you Doc...u numb one." I stood up ready to leave and asked him, "Ting...you want to come to the boats with me?" Ting kind of snickered and laughed. Again I said, "You wanna go with me?"A smile slowly started to come over Ting's face, as if struggling to believe me. "You mean it Doc...you mean it?" "Come on...grab your shit...let's go!" Ting was bursting with excitement and quickly fumbled to grab his gear. He went inside his hooch and said good-bye to his family, promising them he would return. As we walked back to the barge Ting was talking a mile a minute with question after question about the mortar barge.

I introduced Ting to the crew and they immediately liked him. With Tex being the gunner onboard and knowing Ting was a mortar lieutenant for the Viet Cong before he turned his allegiance to the United States, Tex took an obvious interest in him. When we walked Ting to the aft of the barge and showed him the 4-Deuce mortar, with a barrel you could stick your leg in, his eyes lit up like a child in a toy store. Tex spent hours going over the guns with Ting, showing him how to make the loads and most importantly, how to keep them clean.

When it was dark I yelled out to Ting, letting him know we were about to play cards and his interest in the guns quickly diminished. Everyone aboard pretty much stopped what they were doing and sat down inside the bunk room with beer, cigarettes and money. We finished up the evening playing poker, getting drunk, filling the air with smoke and exchanging insults for conversation. Before we hit the bunks that night, I went up top next to the machine gun looking out over the harbor and smoked a few joints with the guys. When the music stopped playing, we stumbled to our bunks.

I got up about 0400 hours and smoked a cigarette while drinking coffee. I talked to Sgt. Owens for a little while, knowing that everything done on the barge was pretty much his show. He was a little straight-laced guy with glasses, dark hair and a slender build. He talked directly to me explaining what goes on during a fire mission. It was his and Sgt. Pound's job inside the map room to take coordinates from over the radio and relay them to Tex, who adjusted and aimed the 4-Deuce mortars. The rest of the crew was responsible for assembling the shells and dropping them into the mortar barrel which, as Sgt. Owens explained to me, was sometimes done at a furious pace, under fire, providing life-saving artillery support for nearby infantry soldiers.

At 0500 our tugboat, with diesel engines rumbling, made its way across the harbor from the Navy dry dock area several hundred yards away. The boat was an LCM-5, a long rectangular craft with an open troop bay for storing our supplies and ammunition. As the boat neared us, it turned around and reversed back within a couple feet of our barge. Tex, a stocky man with a shaved head, threw a rope to one of the men aboard the LCM-5. The tugboat was unique with an elevated cockpit and foot pedals to steer it, allowing the boat's captain to use a weapon and still steer the boat at the same time.

As we were being pulled out into the Song My Tho River to meet up with the rest of the assault force, everyone did their job preparing for the mission ahead. Sgt. Owens and Sgt. Pounds were in the coordinates room looking at maps. Tex was cleaning his mortar guns. Geloski, Padden, Richardson and Capitano were preparing the charges and shells. Sandy and I sat on top of the barge with his dog Hombre. I would have been more than happy to help the crew prepare for the mission, but as their medic, still with a healing leg wound, the crew was deadset on me not lifting a finger.

When I saw the convoy of Tango boats idling in the water, it brought back the all too familiar dreadful memories of being with the 2nd Platoon and the men that fought and died beside me. I knew in one of the three Tango boats was Sgt. Williams, Freeman and Washington. I heard that Roy Moseman had returned as a squad leader. I was sure glad I wasn't going with them. The front of the convoy was led by an Alpha boat, followed next in line by a Monitor—the battleship of our convoy. Staying close to the rear of the Monitor, in front of the Tangos, was the Command and Control boat where the company commander studied the mission ahead of us. As the boats passed us by, the LCM-5 pulled us into the column behind the Tango boats. Then, loaded with enormous fire power, the second Alpha boat in our taskforce fell in behind us. Once our convoy was assembled, all of the boats accelerated with roaring diesel engines, clouding us in a fog of thick diesel fumes.

It was a short voyage passing hundreds of villagers in sampan boats. Several were pulled over by the small, versatile Navy PBR boats to check for identification and weapons caches. The waterway was a busy place, like the streets of an American city, but the native vessels always saw us coming and gave our convoy plenty of room to pass. Any ships that remotely looked like they were not getting out of our way were immediately pulled over by the patrol boats to ensure our convoy wasn't attacked or booby-trapped with a floating mine. When the Tango boats neared the LZ, the LCM-5 pulling our barge separated from the convoy, bringing us to the shoreline. Ed Padden, a tall husky Italian and Goloski, another tall big guy, lowered the heavy wooden gangplank onto the muddy shore. Tex walked the plank and set up two aiming stakes in the ground which gave us a reference point during a fire mission, ensuring us if the barge moved in the water, we would be aware of it. If the barge slipped downstream in the river just a few feet, it could change our mortar trajectory enough to where we would miss the enemy position, or even worse—we could start shelling our own infantry in the field. After setting up the aiming stakes, we were ready to give close fire support for the infantry troops being unloaded about 300 yards up river.

Within minutes after we arrived, dozens of curious Vietnamese children swarmed along the shoreline. Ting began talking to them in his native language, warning them not to get too close to the boats. There were too many horror stories floating around Vietnam about young kids tossing hand-grenades at Americans and running, sometimes even blowing themselves up. With the village being so close to Dong Tam and also having the infantry near us, we felt secure in the area.

As routine, our mission also included going into the village to gather intelligence and feel out the villagers, which was the main reason we needed Ting. After a few minutes of talking with the villagers, Ting knew if there were Viet Cong in the area. Even if the people didn't tell him the enemy was in the vicinity, Ting picked it out in their nervousness and fearful eyes. Ting knew most of the Village chiefs in the Dong Tam area who usually would just come out and tell him if Viet Cong were around.

Sgt. Owens decided to send a squad into the village and of course, I went along as the medic. We stepped down the gangplank and immediately the little children came to our side, knowing that we always handed out candy and chocolate. In the back of the crowd I noticed a boy about twelve years old that was crippled and was being pushed to the side. He fell several times, but managed to stand again. I asked Ting what was wrong with him, and he said it was some kind of arthritis.

As I watched the other children badger him, a sense of compassion came over me and I wanted to help him in some way. I asked Sgt. Owens if I could let the boy carry my rifle for me and he allowed it. As we made our way toward the village, the dozens of children continued to fuss beside us, playing, laughing and eating the candy we gave them while the crippled boy struggled to keep up. We stopped walking and the entire crowd hesitated to see what we were about to do. We turned to the boy and Ting yelled out in Vietnamese for him to come over to us. The other children stood in silence, wondering why we wanted him. As Ting asked him if he could carry my rifle for me, I un-shouldered and unloaded my M-16, and with a breathtaking look, with wide eyes, he stood tall, grabbed my gun and slung it over his shoulder.

Ting and I continued to walk into the village, but at a slower pace so the boy could keep up. For the first time, all the other children fell in behind him. He walked in slow choppy steps with knobby little legs, but his back was straight as an arrow and his head was high. He didn't smile much at first, but Ting gave him a gentle push and he relaxed with a grin.

I finished up handing out medicine and giving vaccination shots. The whole time my new friend held my gun beside me, standing tall on his feeble, arthritic legs. The other children gathered around me and had stopped blackballing the crippled boy. It was late in the evening and Ting's intelligence told us there were no Viet Cong in the area. Sgt. Owens and a couple of men monitored the radio on the barge.

As the sun began to set, we huddled around a fire with the village chief eating a Vietnamese dish and drinking rice whiskey while Ting told funny stories. While all the other children laughed, the crippled boy stood motionless holding my gun like a Roman centurion. We talked a few hours with the village chief and headed back to the barge, spending the rest of the night playing cards and smoking grass.

We returned to the village several times over the course of the next few weeks. It never took me long to find my little buddy. He no longer hobbled in the back, but led the children to greet us. I always handed him my gun and gave him a light slap on the back, along with a gift bag of candy and aspirin for his parents. One of the last times in the village, I brought him aboard the mortar barge. Sgt. Owens was pissed, but the smile on the child's face was priceless. He was the only villager who ever set foot inside our barge.

After operating several weeks in the Dong Tam area, the entire flotilla of the Mobile Riverine Force headed south toward the City of Can Tho. I didn't know what was going on, but it was obvious Viet Cong must have been spotted somewhere for the flotilla to pull anchor and head south. We followed behind the Tango boats once again. Alpha boats rumbled fore and aft of the convoy. In the ranks were a couple of Monitors, ready to unleash their massive firepower. The canal was about seventy yards wide when we broke off from the convoy. It was dark and I could only hear an Alpha boat patrolling to the rear of our position. We pulled into shore next to a small ARVN post with a tiki bar beside it.

Ting went ahead and talked with the villagers and came back with a smile saying, "No VC." We tied off and everyone went into the bar, leaving a GI named Sam to stay in the LCM-5 to monitor the radio. The bar was stilted over the water, packed with ARVN soldiers and oriental women. The building was made of long reeds of grass, interwoven between bamboo poles. Kerosene lanterns lit the bar. Weathered picnic tables provided seating on the deck out over the water.

We were in there for about 2 hours. Being drunk was an understatement for our condition. Tex with his heavyset frame and arms started singing, "God didn't make little green apples," and the second he said apples his hand struck a kerosene lantern, turning the place into a burning inferno. People scratched and clawed their way out of the bar and we raced back to the boats, yelling, "Sam get us the fuck out of here." He throttled up the engines as we scrabbled aboard. We pulled away from the bar full throttle, but never untied from the pier. From the barge, I looked back and saw the ball of fire falling into the canal and the bamboo we tied off to skipping across the water.

The next day, as our convoy came back out of the canal, we passed by where the bar once stood. The only thing left was a couple of bamboo poles sticking out of the water. We kept our guilty eyes forward as we passed by the remnants of the bar. Ting had brought a lot of fun to the barge, without him, we would have had no choice but to stay on high alert. Not once was Ting wrong about Viet Cong being in the area. Ting had relatives all over the delta and knew when someone was lying to him. He could tell if a village was infiltrated with guerillas by the fear in their eyes. Many times after Ting gave the go ahead, we would pull a raft behind the barge and surf, pissing off Sgt. Owens a little; but our crew was mostly seasoned veterans with purple hearts and we were not very easily tamed. We didn't give a shit about anything but each other.

We lived in the here and now, not knowing what a day might bring. Another thing we did to pass the time was make a diving board by taking the gangplank and putting it on top of the barge, weighing the one end down with 50 cal. ammunition boxes, leaving the other end hanging over the water. We went as far as having a diving Olympics between the GI's on the barge and Sandy's boys on the LCM-5.

It was not always fun and games. When a fire mission came in over the radio, it was asses and elbows, but everyone knew their job. Sandy's dog Hombre would hide for cover, trying to avoid the ear splitting guns. Sgt. Owens and Sgt. Pounds would yell out coordinates from down under; Tex would take them and aim the mortars. A couple of guys would prepare the loads and a couple more would drop them in the mortar tubes and always, someone was up on the 50 cal. in case we were attacked. We would pop smoke over the infantry ashore with marking rounds and if the riverine troops liked the placement, they would return over the radio, "Fire for effect"—then the work began.

It was continuous loading of two earth shaking 4-Deuce mortars. The 4-Deuces rested in sand pits to help cushion the recoil of the guns. After a fire mission the barge was covered from stem to stern in sand and during the monsoon rains the sand was like mud, leaving us covered from head to toe. We drew cartoons on the mortar rounds and wrote innuendos like, "Fuck you Charlie." As much as we screwed off in the down time, we took the job serious. Most of us aboard the barge came from the Tango boats and knew how sweet it was to be relieved by fire support in combat. It was a good feeling for me, knowing I was helping those poor bastards out in the bush. I often thought about the guys from my old 2nd Platoon. I knew most had been wounded or killed, but Sgt. Williams, Roy Moseman, Bobby Freeman and James Washington were still with the platoon. When our barge was being pulled behind the Tango boats, I couldn't help but think of them just a few boats in front of me.

Ting and I were already close friends, but after several months on the barge together our friendship became real tight, like the friendship I had with Tom Ziehm. We were all close, surfing and jumping off the diving board together; we had become a family. We drank, smoked grass and pulled burning bars into the water. It was a time in our lives when nothing but survival mattered. Perhaps in a combat zone, without boyish fun, we may have gone insane.

4 Deuce mortar barge, Doc's new home after being wounded a second time in the leg. Below is Doc loading a mortar.

Summer of 68

Summer approached and as part of the 4th and 47th we were placed on airmobile and moved into the barracks inside Dong Tam. The deafening fire missions had made Sandy's dog Hombre crazy with shell shock and eventually the dog started having long episodes of shaking and convulsing, probably due to the concussion of the 4-Deuce mortars. One night Sandy brought him to me inside our gun bunker with tears in his eyes, asking if I could take care of him. I knew what he meant, and after we all gave Hombre one last kiss good-bye, I gave the dog a little more morphine than his body could handle. We thought it was fitting, and in sadness, we let Hombre float away down the Song My Tho River, a river he had traveled with us for hundreds of miles.

Our company took many casualties and lost several men that summer of 1968. Sgt. 1st class Albert Kaiwi Akamu was decapitated by a delayed fused grenade during a demolition procedure on the

259

9th of May 1968. Private James Washington who I had become good friends with was killed on June 6, 1968, by a booby trap, during an AO mission around Dong Tam.

On August 12th, 1968 my company engaged the Viet Cong once again sustaining severe casualties. The men of the 2nd Platoon that were killed that night were: Freddie Lewis, age 20 from Alexandria, LA; Earnest Eatman Jr., age 20, from Birmingham AL; Donald Eugene Pragman, age 23 from Higginsville, MO; Edmond Ray (Red) Toler, age 26 from Goldboro, NC; Leon David Willard, age 20 from Christiansburg, VA; and also my beloved Platoon Sgt. James A. Williams of Paducah, Kentucky.

To make things worse, Roy Moseman recalled:

"When we got back to the ships, I found out that my good friend from Georgia, Bobby Freeman had gotten on a chopper to fly to Saigon to have his eyes checked and the chopper crashed, killing everyone on board. There seemed to be no end to the dying."

Sgt. Williams and Roy Moseman were both awarded the Silver Star for their actions that day. Three days later on the 15th of August, Roy Moseman found himself on another mission. Everything went pretty smooth with little or no contact with the Viet Cong. It was a dull routine operation. On August 16th, the Tango boats came to pick them up. When they got on the boats they were told to go to the back and get down. The boats had been receiving sniper fire and VC had been spotted in the area. Moseman said:

"We had not gone far when all of a sudden there was a loud explosion, a big ball of fire, and a hell of a concussion. My body was vibrating all over. I felt like a tuning fork. The vibration stopped suddenly and I was hurting all over, especially in my right bicep. We had been ambushed and our boat was hit with a B-40 rocket. The rocket hit the top canopy of our boat. The explosion set off some hand grenades and ammunition stored in the front of the boat. I had been hit in the right arm, the left arm, both legs and the mouth. I had also been hit in the face by pieces of plastic from the boat seats. I held my right arm with my left hand and watched the blood puddle up on my chest. It was coming from my mouth. My face was hurting real bad and I thought it had been torn up. One of the Navy crewmembers started working on my wounds. I asked him if my face was real bad and all he would say was, "You're going to be ok." This really scared me since we were always told to never tell someone that was hurt bad, how bad they are. It turned out it was just a lot of blood coming from my mouth and I had two black eyes and some bruises from the plastic seat pieces that hit me in the face. I was much better off than Pat Salerno. When I looked down, I saw Salerno lying on the floor of the boat with one leg blown off and many other shrapnel wounds. As it turned out, five or six more of our men were wounded including Dave Shoenian, Ken Rutkowski, Lt. Charles

261

Rousey, Lannis Janssen and a couple more that I can't remember."

The Navy pulled an Alpha boat up next to the Tango boat the wounded men were in—the Alpha was much quicker for evacuating the wounded. After they were loaded, they were taken to another medical boat outfitted with a helicopter landing pad and were evacuated to Dong Tam. It was Roy Moseman's third Purple Heart. He never returned to the field again. I thought about him a lot over the years, especially the day we were both wounded, covered in each other's blood, running for the same chopper to get the hell out.

The death of Sgt. Williams was staggering for me and the men that knew him. He saved many lives with his knowledge. I still remember his red handkerchief blowing in the wind, flying in a helicopter, standing before me. I can still hear him bragging about his brand new car back home and see his face inside the CP at night, talking with him and Lt. Dimagard. I can hear his voice when we unloaded the Tango boats saying, "Un-ass this mother fucker." Roy Moseman and I both knew how much Sgt. Williams loved his wife. Roy Moseman said that just days before his death he had come back from seeing her on R&R. The first thing out of his mouth was, "She is the most beautiful woman I ever put my eyes on." Sgt. Williams never saw his wife again. At the heart of my memories, I remember honoring him inside Dong Tam, looking at his boots, helmet and rifle, under the melody of Taps.

When I first came to Charlie Company the 2nd Platoon was filled with fresh, young fighting men. The faces became familiar to me and I quickly grew to love them all as brothers. By the end of that summer of 1968, after Moseman was wounded and Washington, Bobby Freeman and Sgt, Williams were killed, I knew no one from my original platoon. Nearly every one of us that had fought for the 2nd Platoon during the Tet Offensive was no longer there. We suffered horrific casualties, sending many of us home with Purple Hearts, and many never made it home at all. In 8 months, we suffered nearly a 100 percent casualty rate. My God!!

Sergeant James A. Williams of Paducah, Kentucky

One More Before You Go

September 1968:

The season of fall showed no promise of peace and we returned to the barge. We had become a family. Our closeness was formed by conversation, but mostly it was created on our bellies in the bottom of the barge with enemy fire bouncing off the vessel, staring each other in the eyes under deafening noise. Without a single word our eyes said, "Get me the fuck out of here my brother." When silence returned, we were so happy to be alive smiles came over our faces. We often settled our nerves and anxiety with a beer and a joint over a game of cards.

The month of August had proven to be a deadly one for our company. As the Senior Medic, I was numb to the bloody dog tags that passed through my hands, too many of the names I had known personally. When Sgt. Williams died, I recall a very real fear came over me. I always looked at Sgt.

Williams as the all knowing man that couldn't be killed; when he died, I realized no one was guaranteed a ticket home alive. For sanity's sake, my emotions became impervious to death.

Along with a full task force of Tango, Alpha and Monitor boats, we headed south again toward the city of Can Tho, stopping to rest near shore to refuel and eat lunch. As we were checking the villagers for proper identification cards, we noticed a sampan sneaking out of the village. Ting yelled in Vietnamese for them to stop, but the escaping boat loaded with people continued on its way into the river. Ting ran to the mortar pit, looked out at the sampan with a glare, checked the distance, and then adjusted the gun. He dropped in a shell and our barge shook with concussion—sending a shell whistling and exploding off the bow of the fleeing boat. Ting looked up again and made another adjustment on the mortar and dropped in the 2nd shell. Within seconds the sampan exploded into flames, leaving bodies and debris sinking and floating in the river. Ting just snickered with a grin, and all of us applauded his accuracy, laughing and saying "Fucking Gooks."

Shortly after the explosion, one of the PBR boats left our convoy to search the debris. They pulled the bodies out of the water with a long hook and threw them in a sampan boat. Women began wailing with tears and the babies soon followed.

Undoubtedly they were family and had to bury the bones of their dead loved ones.

There were no opinions about the women that died aboard. Whether the women were guilty or hijacked, it didn't matter to me, they were dead anyways. That is how I justified the chaos with my mind—"the dead no longer suffered." I had seen a woman machine gunner shoot a friend of mine, so as to "Who could kill you?" gender did not matter in the Nam. I hated them because they were shooting at me, but that was about it. It wasn't a deep hatred against their beliefs or the color of their skin. I was purely trying to survive, wanting to see my family once again. When Ting killed those people it didn't matter to me in the least, I knew that no children were in the boat.

We continued toward the South China Sea near Can Tho, in response to the movement of enemy forces from Cambodia, then into the southern most parts of Vietnam. It had been over 8 months since the Tet Offensive and the thousands of disbanded Viet Cong seemed to be making resurgence in the Mekong Delta. For the first few days of the operation the threat of the enemy was very small. We spent the nights playing cards and drinking Zuday whiskey. One night after everyone hit the bunks, a new guy that replaced Sgt. Pounds got up to take a piss and fell overboard. In the morning, after putting many miles behind us, we noticed he was gone. I never saw him again and often wonder to this day if he made it home.

For the most part the river was wide as we sailed through the delta. But like clockwork, when the shores narrowed, the enemy was waiting with hit and run ambushes. Usually the ambushes consisted of a few pot shots with B-40 rockets, but on one occasion they managed to blow a helicopter off a medical evacuation boat. Somebody was always dying or getting wounded—when it wasn't happening right in your lap, death was always within eyesight.

The trip to Can Tho was one of my last missions. I then considered myself a short-timer, with less than two months left in the Nam. The Riverine Force was throwing nearly everything we had south. The convoy of ships seemed endless, bending through the river like a snake. The villagers and fishermen watched with dread from inside their sampans and fishing boats. The tiny boats swayed in our wake.

We must have had a battalion's worth of infantrymen in the Tango boats. There was a flamethrower, a Tango fitted with a helicopter deck, and more heavies and Alpha boats than I had ever seen together. The barge behind us was fitted with 105 Howitzers. The mission down to Can Tho was a long one. I had an uneasy feeling and when we finally reached the city it looked like home, with

Chevrolets and other cars driving down paved roads, pulling in and out of a Texaco gas station.

The river was about 150 yards wide as we neared the bridge and standing on the bridge were ARVN marines holding rifles. Sandy's crew in the LCM-5 pulled us under and I remember looking back at a small pocket platform on the bridge and seeing a soldier standing there. The most prevalent sounds were our diesel engines.

We got about seventy yards past the bridge and all hell broke loose. We started taking fire from both sides of the river. Rockets, machine gun fire and small arms hit us hard. I could see the rockets exploding in the water all around the convoy. Then with a deafening blast a rocket hit the side of our barge, throwing me off my feet. Smoke was everywhere, but the steel plating did its job and no one was injured. Bullets continued to ricochet off our barge like a rainstorm.

Within seconds the 105's behind us lowered their cannons, throwing beehive rounds point blank into the shore of the city. I knew Sandy got behind the 50 caliber up top, but all I heard was the 105's deafening blast. Our heavies and Alphas let go with all they had and on both sides of us. The city was turned into a chaos of burning structures and explosions. The inferno forced hundreds of people into the water, fleeing from burning boats and burning buildings. The fuel on the water ignited into flames and I could see people trying to swim through the fire toward our boats. I aimed at them, killing them, we all did. I could smell burning flesh and gas as the air became thick with smoke. The smoke floated in the air with the wind, but in cloudless pockets I could see people's faces in the water. Then the smoke would cover them again. Some of the faces were engulfed in flames and others were pinkish with singed hair or no hair at all. The flowing smoke again revealed floating bodies and people swimming in the water burning with fire. The excruciating screams could be heard between the blasts of the Howitzers. After a couple of minutes I noticed some of the people in the water were children. Several were brought aboard the PBR boats for medical attention, but most didn't make it through the burning fuel in the water.

The bustling city streets had been devoured. Our convoy never stopped moving until we put the city behind us and the gun fire stopped. When it was over, I looked back at the city in awe at the destruction we unleashed. I was shaken by the death and carnage. I witnessed with my own eyes the unveiling of power held inside a barge full of 105 Howitzers. It was unreal—unfucking believable. There was nothing left of Can Tho's waterfront that was without damage or completely destroyed.

Our convoy rested outside the city limits and unloaded the infantry at a nearby firebase. The quick but vicious battle left the men on the barge quiet. During the night I climbed the ladder and sat down next to the 50 cal. machine gun. I sat there looking up at the sky and prayed to God. After praying I glanced toward the city and could see its glow, wondering if it was the city lights or if it still burned.

After a several days of providing artillery support to airmobile and riverine troops, we turned around and started the long voyage back to Dong Tam. As it turned out—the Viet Cong had opened fire from behind the city. Much of the dead were civilians. The entire operation was a wash, leaving a devastating set back to the City of Can Tho. The "Old Reliable" newspaper, reported that it set the war back years.

As we moved closer to Dong Tam, it became harder and harder for me to believe I had survived almost an entire year of that shit. Under the rumbling engines and the swishing sound of splitting water, our boats made the voyage back. I felt fear return inside me. I hadn't felt fear like that since my first time in combat. I knew I was entering the Dong Tam harbor for the last time aboard a barge when Sgt. Owens gave word we were staying in Dong Tam for airmobile support.

I spent my last few weeks in base camp. They were the longest days of my life. I drank and smoked marijuana inside the bunker we had turned into a bar. I literally lived in a bunker for weeks, petrified even to go take a shit. I felt fear build inside me those last days; it was like I almost couldn't even move.

With only a handful of days left in the Nam, one of Charlie Company's platoons was hit bad while pulling security for an airstrip. Some Officer requested that I be immediately shipped out to the platoon. I was breathless with fear. The past several weeks I had been giving shots and working with Doc Stillman, who was one of the head doctors in Dong Tam. When he heard about the request for me, he put an end to it. He told the requesting officer, "MacSwan has seen enough… he's unfit for duty." I will always remember Doc Stillman doing that for me.

The day I left everyone was on duty. I walked to the airstrip by myself that day. In the air the plane banked to the side and I watched Dong Tam fade in the distance, but never would it fade in my memory. I felt many emotions, love for my brothers and hate for the Nam. There was a very real sense that part of me was still there and would always remain there. It was like a part of me had died. Waiting for me was a weight that could never be measured; the heaviness of a world filled with spitting protestors and decontamination showers. A world so incredibly upside down it thought, "Your home now…it's all over."

Epilogue

Five decades have passed since the war. Sometimes it's hard for me to imagine that my father was there at all. His youth seems so long ago, running underneath a hail of gunfire, with rockets and mortars exploding, spitting mud and covering him in filth. His emotions had become impervious to death. Today at 71 years old, he can hardly handle the sight of a suffering bird.

In the winter of 2001 he received a telephone call from Tom Ziehm. They hadn't talked to each other since they said good-bye on the mortar barge in Vietnam. They talked for hours about how life treated them and relived several memories from the war. Tom had joined the police force shortly after his return and had spent his lifetime hunting and fishing. They had both lived very similar lives. It wasn't long after their telephone conversation began, that they realized they needed to see one another.

Within a few weeks Tom and his wife Theresa came out to see my dad. When he stepped out of the car, Tom looked nothing like the tall slender man I knew from my dad's photographs. After 33 years the two neared each other and embraced. We all sat down in some lawn furniture and my dad and Tom began talking. It wasn't awkward in the least. In a certain sense it was as if they had stayed in contact through the years. As Tom showed us his fishing and deer hunting albums my dad began to notice the old mannerisms he once knew, now decades after the war. It was like they recognized each other at the same time; the talking ceased, their eyes filled with tears and they embraced again. After 3 decades since Vietnam, time itself was powerless to the closeness of their brotherhood. The two soldiers went about their own lives after the war, but as old age crept in, the love could no longer be ignored.

After thinking about my dad all his life, when Tom learned that he was sick, my dad (Doc) MacSwan was the first person he wanted to see. He wished he didn't have to see Tom so feeble, having known him as such a strong young man and great leader. I suppose it was better than to never see him again at all.

A short time had passed after Tom left for home when his wife called. She said Tom didn't have much time left and he wanted to see my dad before he died. He went out to Michigan and entered his home and was greeted by Bruce (Moose) Johnson at the foot of Tom's bed. The three Super troopers were together again. My dad and Bruce talked with Tom for a little while, but Tom was nearly too weak to say much. My dad felt an urge to try and help him, but there were no bullet wounds for him to patch up. When it was time to go, they looked at him and my dad said, "Tom, you take the point and Bruce will follow you, I'll cover you both." Tom responded to him with a weak grin.

Only hours after Moose and my dad left on April 11, 2001, Tom Ziehm took the point and was the first of the three Super troopers to go into the unknown of death. His sickness was called "Good Pastures Syndrome," believed to be linked to Agent Orange. That was one wound my dad could not treat. To this day he thanks God for having those last few moments with his brother. The name Tom Ziehm will be said in our household for generations to come. I will hold his name high, along with the others.

When my dad is in his deer stand and he closes his eyes while waiting for daylight, he can still see Tom's shadowy figure moving through the moonlight, leading a platoon of men across a rice paddy. He can still see Tom's face, as they ate the box of cookies the night my dad was wounded in the leg and he can still see his tall slender frame walking away from the barge after saying their good-byes.

I think back as far as I can remember; I see my dad throwing a football to me and playing with my sisters. I remember him teaching us how to fish for largemouth bass, using a Texas-style rubber worm. He showed me the way of the woods, hunting the elusive whitetail deer and stressing the importance of a good clean shot, not leaving an animal wounded. He taught me that if a life was to be taken, it should never be wasted.

I now understand that sometimes while being a father or out on the bass waters or in the woods, his mind was often somewhere else. His silence left much unsaid. He battled many demons heroically inside his soul.

He has had many dreams and nightmares of the war, but there is only one place he told me he ever actually flashed back. There is a place south of the city of Buffalo, a small village called Java, where I once hunted with my dad many years ago. For years we parked the car on the side of the road, and then trudged off into the snow. Sometimes the fresh lake effect snow off Lake Erie was so deep it was up to my waist and I struggled to keep up in my dad's footsteps. There was a steep hill we climbed and at the top was an old barbed wire fence, but we found a place to cross where it had been damaged. It was there, when my dad would pause before stepping out into the open field, we sometimes stood for several minutes before crossing, heading deep inside the distant hardwoods. It wasn't until a couple years ago, while working on this book, my dad confided in me, telling me, when he paused there at the top of the hill, he had flashed back to Vietnam. It wasn't a horrific flash like many have had; it was just him standing on the edge of a rice paddy, looking out at a distant tree line of palms. No bullets or explosions, only the dreadful feeling that all combat soldiers feel inside when they near a distant tree-line. It occurred to him that in all these years, few have ever really known him as the Combat Medic who fought for our country.

I look at all the old photographs after he came back from the war, the early Harley Davidson years, restoring antique cars, coaching football, hunting and fishing, and realize he must have held a lot of feelings inside, locking the madness away, so he could function as a father and in society itself. He told me he is grateful to have a mind strong enough to block out the horror.

While writing this book with my dad, I understand why the outdoors has entranced his soul all these years, sometimes causing him to be labeled as a near hermit. Could it be that nature expects nothing from us, except one thing—survival? It doesn't care who you are or how much money you have. All nature requires is that you sustain life and if you are still enough, she will reveal herself to you. The year 1968 required three things of my dad the medic: survive; sustain life; and, save those who could be saved around him.

House mortgages, bills, fancy cars, clothing and everything else didn't mean shit, yet when he returned from the war these trappings of the world pressed down upon him. Indeed he wanted a normal life and the strong mind of his youth was able to bury his anger for spoiled America, anger toward those that ranted and raved when things didn't go their way, rather than being grateful for simply being alive in the moment.

I suppose for a while he wanted all the protestors and politicians to know what it was like to be in a firefight and to hold dying men, women and children in their arms. For a few years after the war those demons didn't go away. He would get out of work and ride his motorcycle drunk and stoned without any fear of death, caring nothing about accomplishments or material possessions. But as years passed by, he became softer and accepting. He was no longer the hardened combat veteran having just lived through a literal hell.

Today he is one of thousands that have lived through the combat of war. I have learned they are part of a sacred brotherhood and have seen more death than a person should have ever seen. As a society we must reaffirm their cause and know that every freedom we possess in this constitutional republic was bled for. We must understand soldiers are not the same as when they left for war. When they get that distant stare, perhaps their minds are in a far away land of jungle or the sands of the Middle

East. When their temper is short—know that deep inside they are battling the question, "Why me...why did I make it?" When they cry during the national anthem before the Super Bowl, know they gave their entire being for America and the constitution—which was not a game. On the 4th of July, when you see their arm hairs stand on end, they will be hearing the terrifying sounds of combat, and when you hear the echo of taps in their presence, and some break down to their knees in tears, it is the dead they see.

Today, over 50 years since my dad returned from the war, with 7 grandchildren, his anger has now silenced. With the silencing of his anger and restless spirit, the memories of the war come back to him. They are mostly good thoughts of playing cards and the smiles of the brothers he once knew, but sometimes his mind takes him back to that horrible place. He doesn't have many visual flash backs, but rather it's flashes of emotions he feels, whether from the death of a soldier on the news, the high explosive smell of rotten eggs, the Mekong smell of vegetation rotting in water or the smell of barbeque beef that was on the lips of Lieutenant Dimagard as my dad tried to resuscitate him. Every once in a while he feels the same dread, as if he was still there. These are scars that the combat soldier carries for a lifetime for us and our freedom.

No one knows when a war will ravage his or her homeland or the form in which the battle will be.

Perhaps the entire world will be engulfed in war. Maybe the remnants of earth will stagger through a land of desolation and pick up this book or yours. Will they say, "We must never do that," thus creating a whole new world of peace?

I don't think so. I believe war will exist, always leaving men, women and children to die. It could be our history will never educate a truly free world; a world without war. It is easier and more logical for me to hope for the help of divine intervention. So we wait for the day of God's vengeance. Children will continue to have heroes gently pulling them out of the rubble of war and carrying them to safety. Standing for God will be the Christian, Jewish, Muslim and other soldiers of The United States of America, all fighting in one Spirit against the tyranny of evil. Until the day when the guns have silenced, America will have her soldiers and the soldiers will have a Combat Medic like my father Doc.

Don (Doc) James MacSwan earned 2 Purple Hearts, a Bronze Star, and the Army Commendation Medal with "V" Device for heroism in connection with military operations against an armed hostile force in the Republic of Vietnam.